'The Widest Circle'
Remembering Michael Sweetman

Michael Sweetman 1935–72

'The Widest Circle'

Remembering
Michael Sweetman

Edited by
Barbara Sweetman FitzGerald

A. & A. Farmar

British Library Cataloguing in Publication Data
A CIP catalogue record for this book is available
from the British Library

ISBN: 978-1-906353-28-5

This edition first published in 2011
by
A. & A. Farmar Ltd
78 Ranelagh Village, Dublin 6, Ireland
Tel +353-1-496 3625 Fax +353-1-497 0107
Email afarmar@iol.ie,
Web www.aafarmar.ie

Printed and bound by Gemini International
Typeset and designed by A. & A. Farmar
Index by Helen Litton

For
Michèle, Caroline, Patrick, Christopher,
Rachel and Timothy

Contents

'The Widest Circle'

The title 'The Widest Circle' is taken from a favourite quotation of Hubert Butler's, from Wolfe Tone's contemporary Lord Charlemont: 'Like circles raised in the water by the impulse of a heavy body, our social duties as they expand grow fainter, and lose in efficacy what they gain in extent . . . The love and service of our country is perhaps the widest circle in which we can hope to display an active benevolence . . . If every man were to devote his powers to the service of his country, mankind would be universally served.'
Hubert Butler, *Wolfe Tone and the Common Name of Irishman*
(The Lilliput Press, Gigginstown, 1985).

Foreword

Mary Robinson*

This book serves a number of purposes. It reminds us of the leadership qualities and contribution of a thirty-six-year-old whose tragic death was also a public loss to Ireland. It is a source of pride and joy to family and friends, who welcome the recognition a beloved figure has been given. It is also a lens through which we recall the Ireland of the 1950s, 1960s and 1970s, and the struggles it went through. It should be an inspiration in the bleak context of an Ireland battered by the financial crisis, and our own foolishness, that values of integrity, intelligent analysis, political courage and a vision for the future are present in every generation and matter more in times of hardship.

The childhood accounts by Michael's brother David and his cousin John Dillon remind me of two visits to Johnsbrook with Michael's sister Mary, my direct contemporary in Mount Anville. I loved the house and grounds, and recall listening in the kitchen to a conversation about bee-keeping between Michael's mother Mimi and her sister Bessie in their rich La Touche accents, which had influenced a family way of speaking which was quite distinctive. Bruce Arnold recalls with affection 'the rich tone of his voice, the fulsome laughter . . .'

Michael was the sophisticated, urbane older brother who shocked me by his knowledge of wine as I wore my pioneer pin with teenage innocence. It was clear that in that family he was looked to, in David's words, as 'the rock on which our family stood.'

Denis Corboy captures well the educational influences they shared

* Mary Robinson was the seventh President of Ireland from 1990 to 1997 after which she became the United Nations High Commissioner for Human Rights based in Geneva. In 2002, she established Realising Rights, based in New York. Returning to Ireland in 2010 she set up the Mary Robinson Foundation—Climate Justice under the Innovation Alliance of Trinity College and University College Dublin.

in Glenstal, and later at University College Dublin, where they studied under Professors Robin Dudley Edwards and Desmond Williams, among others. They also became involved in the youth branch of the European Movement, which would influence both their future careers.

Unlike Michael, I did not come from a political family. But when I began to champion liberal causes, and was elected to the Senate in August 1969, I found in Michael an honesty of thought and a rounded political judgment reflected in his work with Declan Costello in *Towards a Just Society* which impressed me deeply. Enda McDonagh, who only met Michael once, describes very well the background of the 1950s, 1960s and early 1970s—'the inadequate distinction between culture and religion, their intermingling at so many levels and in so many areas of life, from the artistic and intellectual to the political and economic, obscured what in neighbouring countries would be sharply differentiated as properly secular and properly religious.' I was still in college during the 1966 Presidential election campaign, but I recall the impact of speeches given by Tom O'Higgins, which Michael had crafted, as described by his cousin John Dillon. He quotes from a position paper Michael had prepared at the time: 'The man we elect as President can play a key role in encouraging this larger, more generous patriotism which belongs to the new, young Ireland emerging today. Only this kind of outlook can lead to reconciliation with our fellow countrymen in the North.'

Garret FitzGerald reminds us of the other strong passion of Michael's life: to help find a solution that would end the violence in Northern Ireland. He accompanied Garret and Tom O'Higgins on a visit to John Hume in late 1969, at the height of the Civil Rights Movement, and in early 1972 they travelled together to 'the shattering funeral of the victims of the British paratroopers in Derry'.

I spent some delightful time in the company of Michael and Tom O'Higgins as we campaigned for Ireland's membership of the EEC. Michael's role in this campaign is well described by Liam Connellan, but I tend to recall the aftermath of serious public debates—often against the passionate advocacy of Justin Keating—when Michael, Tom O'Higgins and Denis Corboy and myself would repair to the bar and have a hilarious time recalling the fine moments of oratory until I would leave the men and retire giggling to my room.

My most vivid memory is of a European Movement meeting—I think in The Hague—which ended with the four of us in Tom's bedroom, he now jacketless and showing traditional braces to hold his trousers up, and regaling us with the funnier moments in his Presidential campaign. How little I knew then of what the future would hold!

During this time of serious campaigning for European membership by day, and relaxing in friendly satire and fun together by night, Michael often spoke with deep affection about Barbara and his children. I had met Barbara with Michael, but had not really got to know her in her own right. Denis, the bachelor, would tease him, and I—then expecting my first child—wondered at how relaxed and loving he was about having six, showing us photos, ranging from the twins Caroline and Michèle aged fourteen to Timmy aged five.

The devastating impact of Michael's death, together with eleven other well-known Irish businessmen, in the Staines air crash on 18 June 1972, as they were on their way to Brussels to make arrangements to establish the Irish Business Bureau, is described by a number of the contributors. I, too, was devastated, and tried to comfort Denis Corboy who had an early sense of guilt as he had planned at one stage to be on that flight.

I called to see Barbara at 20 Park Drive, Ranelagh, and thus began one of the strongest friendships of my life. Her inner strength and spirituality helped me, and so many others, to cope with what was a lesser but still painful grief. I found myself going back to Park Drive almost every day over that summer, really getting to know Caroline, Michèle, Patrick, Christopher (Kip), Rachel and Timmy. By September I had asked Barbara to become godmother to Tessa, born on 2 October 1972. Barbara's joy in her birth was somehow an affirmation that life must go on.

An early public manifestation of the affection and esteem in which Michael was held by a wide circle of friends and admirers was the establishment in 1975 of the Michael Sweetman Educational Trust, with its essay competition and scholarships, encouraging younger generations of Irish students, North and South, to pursue their interest in European issues.

The publication of this book will ensure that future generations will understand his place in Irish history, and the enormous potential which sadly was unable to be realised.

I hope these personal accounts and reflections will bring joy to Barbara and members of the immediate and wider family, and that they will inspire younger readers to the ideals of a just society and a new way to live together on the island of Ireland, which were at the core of Michael's vision.

Introduction

Barbara Sweetman FitzGerald*

As Michael would have been 75 in 2010 I thought this would be a good time to edit a book in his memory. Among the 118 people killed in the Staines air crash on 18 June 1972 were 12 Irish businessmen: all had a promising future, for themselves and the country, before them. I hope I will be forgiven for singling Michael out. He was one of the youngest to be killed and had already achieved a lot in his short life. I wanted his children and his grandchildren to know more about him. Family memories are often glamourised so I wanted to record the views of others who had known him.

We had met in University College Dublin in the mid-fifties. We were married by my first cousin Dom Wulfstan Phillipson OSB from Downside Abbey on 5 March 1957. (After the crash he offered to educate the boys at Downside and though my mother and my sister had been educated in England I felt those days were past and declined.) We were to have left Dublin on a Greek shipping line vessel that night to emigrate to Canada, but its anchor had got entangled which meant a few days in Wicklow, first in Hunter's Hotel and then in Michael's uncle Hugh's house, Derrybawn, in Glendalough. When in Hunter's Hotel many years later I noted that the number of the bedroom in which we had slept was fifteen, the number of years we had had together. We were fortunate that Michael had an uncle

---

* Barbara Sweetman FitzGerald was born in Dublin and educated at the Convent of the Sacred heart, Leeson Street. She left UCD to marry Michael Sweetman at the age of twenty and graduated some thirty years later from Trinity College Dublin with a BA Hons degree in History of Art. She was the first woman to be appointed to the board of the ESB in 1973. Involved with different charities over the years she ran Breadline Africa when it was first set up in Ireland. She was awarded an honorary CBE in 2001 for her work with the Irish Association for Cultural, Economic and Social Relations, the first North/South reconciliation body. She is a patron of the British Irish Association.

then living in Montreal. Through David La Touche I got a job in an advertising agency. About the second week I was there my boss asked how Michael was doing. When I told him he was about to take a job in a department store selling shoes he said 'send him in to me'. The result was Michael became an advertising executive while I became the media buyer.

Those fifteen years were years of great happiness. We moved from Montreal back to Ireland in 1959, when our twin daughters were eighteen months old. Our first son Patrick was born in Dublin. Two years later we returned to Montreal where Christopher was born. Michael was now with Córas Tráchtála (CTT—the Irish Export Board), running their Montreal office. The following year he was asked to move to New York to run CTT's office there. Rachel was born in New York in December, 1962. We returned to Ireland for good in the spring of 1963: four years later Timothy was born in Dublin.

Michael and I shared many interests, including Northern Ireland. Nineteen-seventy-two was the year of Bloody Sunday when thirteen people were killed in Derry by the British army.

The memory of this tragedy and the memory of many happy years was what sustained me after the crash. Why should I be spared when so many others had suffered the loss of loved ones? I knew how fortunate I was to have had so many years of happiness.

While at UCD I remember walking up Kildare Street with Michael. He looked across at Leinster House and said: 'Don't let me go into politics'. He knew it was in his blood. Our wedding day was the day of a general election when Fine Gael went out of office. My father was very amused when Gerard Sweetman's mother apologised for his non-attendance by saying he was the Chancellor of the Exchequer! As soon as we returned from New York Michael became involved with Fine Gael.

Many chapters in this book are concerned with Fine Gael connections which very much became part of my life. In 1974 I was fortunate to marry Alexis FitzGerald whose wife Grace Costello had died in the same year as Michael. We each had six children; two of Alexis' were already married, so we had ten in the house. It was not easy—losing a parent is so very difficult—but we all survived and I would like to pay tribute to the love and kindness I continue to receive from my stepchildren. Both Michael and Alexis, who died in 1985, would be amused by the connections of my two youngest grandchildren, Ralph and Jemima. My daughter Michèle met her husband David Sutton when David's sister Isabelle married Andrew Dillon who had been my pageboy all those years ago. David and Isabelle's grandfather John A. Costello is my stepchildren's grandfather and Ralph and Jemima's great-grandfather.

I am grateful to Roy Foster for finding a title for the book. The quotation is taken from a book by Hubert Butler, *Wolfe Tone and the Common Name of Irishman* and was a favourite quote of Butler's from Lord Charlemont. I like the idea of a circle encompassing the activities of one's life. It seems apposite to apply it to Michael who had so many interests and strove hard 'to devote his powers to the service of his country'. I also like the connection with Hubert Butler. Hubert and Peggie Butler were very fond of Michael. I remember many good discussions at Maidenhall, their home in Kilkenny. In particular, after the death of Peggie's brother, Tyrone, there was much chat about how best to ensure their family home at Annaghmakerrig, Co. Monaghan, would become a residence for writers and artists. It is now long established as the Tyrone Guthrie Centre with which I am happy to be involved.

I would like to thank all those who have helped with the book. I am grateful to my publishers Tony and Anna Farmar for their kindness and patience and for putting up with my lack of expertise on the computer, my daughter Caroline, who conducted the interviews with Donal Flynn, Brendan Halligan and, most fortunately, with Jim Dooge not long before he died, and my son Patrick who helped transcribe Michael's writings and also with great patience, deciphered a sea-damaged document. This document was the text of a speech given by Michael on St Patrick's Day, 1963 to the New York Athletic Club which gives an example of how little understood Ireland was by the United States at that time. Special thanks are due to Ciara Meehan, James McGuire and Ruth Dudley Edwards for their help in editing some chapters and also to an old friend who wishes to remain anonymous but gave much of that precious commodity, 'time'.

Michael Sweetman's ancestors

Charles Lysaght*

Michael Sweetman belonged to a Catholic family longer established in prosperity than most of their co-religionists. They
were unusual among families of their social background, Catholic or
otherwise, in the fullness of their participation in the political and
professional life of post-independence Ireland.

Their documented descent begins with successful brewers in 18th-
century Dublin who took part in the struggle to remove the penal
laws affecting 'Papists'; Patrick Sweetman (a direct ancestor) and John
Sweetman were members of the Catholic Convention of 1792. John's
later involvement in the United Irishmen led to his being exiled in
France until his death in 1826.

Patrick's son Michael carried on the brewery from its final premises in Francis Street (now the Iveagh Markets) into the second half
of the 19th century. Michael married in 1802 as his first wife, Alice
Taaffe of Smarmore Castle in Co Louth, a member of a dispossessed
Catholic family whose fortunes were reviving. Before his death in
1852 he acquired the Longtown Estate near Sallins in County Kildare
(eventually inherited by Gerard Sweetman, the Fine Gael Minister
for Finance). Michael's eldest son, another Patrick, was High Sheriff
of Kildare in 1862 and also Deputy Lieutenant of the county.

Although Patrick's first cousin John Sweetman, of Drumbarrow
near Kells, was a nationalist MP in the 1890s and subsequently a
founding member of Sinn Féin (and incidentally, progentitor of the
Republican and Fianna Fáil Sweetmans), there seems to have been no

---

* Charles Lysaght was a consultant to the editors of *Burke's Irish Family Records*
(1976) and a contributor to the *Dictionary of Irish Biography* (2009). His publications
include *Brendan Bracken: A Biography* (1979), *Edward McLysaght, A Memoir* (1986),
Great Irish Lives (2008).

political involvement among Michael's direct ancestors until Patrick's son Hugh's son Roger, born in 1874, was returned for North Wexford as a Sinn Féin candidate in the General Election of 1918, defeating by a fair margin Sir Thomas Grattan Esmonde of the Irish Party. As such, Roger Sweetman was a member of the first Dáil established by Sinn Féin in the aftermath of that election.

Unlike many of his fellow candidates he was not in prison and so was able to attend the inaugural meeting of the Dáil at the Mansion House in January 1919. However, he resigned from Sinn Féin in protest against the subsequent campaign of violence and was not a member of the second Dáil elected in 1921. He had inherited an estate in Dunlavin from his uncle Edmund Casimir Sweetman, the eldest brother of his father's generation (who had been married to the sister of General Sir William Butler) and who died without issue in 1913 leaving assets worth £150,000.

Roger Sweetman lived in Derrybawn House, Glendalough, and was a Knight of Magistral Grace in the Irish Association of the Order of Malta. He married in 1904 Kathleen Aliaga Kelly and had eleven children, one of whom Edmund, a barrister, was active in Fine Gael politics as a senator before becoming a Land Commisisioner, while two were in religion, Michael as a Jesuit, and Joan as a nun of the Sacred Heart Order.

Roger's eldest child Patrick, educated at Mount St Benedict near Gorey where a cousin, Dom Francis Sweetman of Downside Abbey was headmaster, qualified as a solicitor and practised in Oldcastle until appointed County Registrar for Meath in 1951 just before the Fine Gael-led coalition left office. He married in 1934 Mimi La Touche, a member of a renowned Huguenot family whose immediate ancestors had become Catholic at the time of the Oxford Movement and had lived out of Ireland for several generations. Michael was the eldest in his family of two sons and four daughters brought up largely at Johnsbrook near Kells, which his parents bought in 1940.

My brother Michael: a personal recollection of the Johnsbrook years

David Sweetman*

Michael was the eldest of six children in our family and was almost three years older than me with my sister Liz between us. Michael, Liz and I spent our first years at Hurdlestown just south of Kells, Co. Meath where my father and mother had moved from Wicklow when my father took up practice as a solicitor in Kells. I was born in April 1938 and Michael in June 1935. We had four sisters Liz, Kate, Mary and Margaret. To me as a child, Michael always appeared to be much older and more sensible and could always be depended on to steer one in the right direction.

In 1941 the family moved to Johnsbrook House, which is just off the road from Kells to Clonmellon (N52), and was a Georgian house that once belonged to the Dashwood-Tandy family. The house had been bought with 30 acres of land for £100 from Matty Lynch who lived at the crossroads of the Athboy/Crossakeel and Kells/Clonmellon roads where they used to play pitch and toss on a Sunday morning for pennies. I still have the letter from my father confirming the financial deal and hoping that they would become good neighbours. At the front and one side of the house were lawns, flower beds etc. and a large greenhouse. There was a fairly long drive which went through a wood of mainly mature trees with some laurel bushes and it was in this wood that we spent much of our free time playing

A small river ran at the bottom of the field to the front of the house which provided a water supply to the house by damming it to

* David Sweetman's career in the National Monuments Service began in 1970. He took over the direction of the Archaeological Survey of Ireland in 1984. As Chief Archaeologist from 1994 until his retirement in 2003 he presided over the expansion of the archaeological service. His book *The Medieval Castles of Ireland* was published in 1999.

give enough of a drop to work a hydraulic dam. The river also divided Johnsbrook from Drewstown House which belonged to the McVeigh family. The river flowed through part of the beech wood and contained small brown trout which I used to catch on night lines. My mother loved these trout but my father was very disapproving of my methods of fishing. The dammed water formed a small lake in which was a small island. The domestic ducks every morning would find their way down to the lake and frequently make nests on the island. Michael and I used to follow them and take my father's small canvas boat out to the island to retrieve the eggs. Swans also every year made nests among the reeds in the lake. Our father was very patient with us and used to take us out on the lake when we were very young and taught us how to fly fish. However I never remember anyone ever catching a trout in the lake. On several occasions my father let the water out of the lake in the summer in order to get the pike out of it. Michael and I were armed with spears which had been made out of flattened nails attached to poles. Michael was always excited by the prospect of the lake being drained but I was not enamoured of the idea of spearing the pike. Michael would then get my mother to stuff and bake a pike for him.

I have only a few early memories of Michael even though we always shared the same room and he always called me Butch. Since he was that much older I seem to have spent more of my time with my three sisters. However I distinctly remember playing with tin model soldiers in the attic of Johnsbrook where we had room to leave our armies in battle formation. We built forts and trenches and lined up our armies to face each other. We then proceeded to throw empty cartridge cases at each other's soldiers with the disastrous consequence of knocking their heads off. They were re-attached using match sticks and glue. We also played games with our soldiers out-of-doors in a small grove to the side of the house where we did our various manoeuvres. Michael was always the master strategist here. I remember once in Donegal on Marble Hill beach Michael set up some of the soldiers and tanks and lit pieces of paper to make it look as if they were under attack. He than took a photo of the scene of devastation with a Brownie camera and with the results we triumphantly told our friends they were pictures of real World War II combat.

I suppose my abiding memory of Michael would be his love of

food, wine and classical music. Before we even had a proper record player, Michael when he was on holidays would often be glued to the classical music on the radio; there was no television in our house at that time. I remember when my father bought *The Messiah* on wax in numerous discs and stacked them one upon the other and when one was finished the next would drop into its place. I now have a fondness for Handel's oratorios but in those days when Michael and my father played his music in the house, I left immediately to play outside.

At the rear of the house was a small enclosed yard in which there was a workhorse, cows, calves and all kinds of poultry. Behind the yard was a walled garden which used the yard buildings as one wall. Michael from early on showed an interest in the fruit, but especially in the trees. When we came home from Donegal at the end of our August holiday every year, the first thing Michael did was to run out to the enclosed garden to see how the apples, pears and plums were doing. Although he ate every vegetable he was more interested in fruit growing, something he retained to the end of his life.

In the early 1950s my father purchased ten acres of land in a place called Beggar's Bush which was just up the road from Johnsbrook for the purpose of grazing and hay-making. One of the immediate advantages to Michael and me was that there were numerous rabbits in the field. We commenced to snare these on a regular basis and sold them to a man with a van called 'The Cleaver' for about one shilling each. The main disadvantage of the ample supply of rabbits was that my mother fed us frequently on them, cooked in every imaginable way.

I remember playing some games with Michael and he and I were very much interested in horses which stemmed from our mother who took us to point-to-point races in Crossakeel and Delvin. Michael once put two shillings and sixpence on a horse at the Delvin races and when he came back to collect his winnings the bookie had run away. The only horse we had on the farm was a mare called Molly and we used to ride her bare-backed around the paddock. We also set up fences in the paddock for jumps for ourselves and had races over them. A long time later when we had come back from Canada we frequently went to race meetings but only those with the highest number of winning favourites. We had a system of doubling our money against favourites which at times became somewhat tense.

My father was born and reared on a farm in Glendalough and was one of five boys. They all fished and went shooting in the hills around Derrybawn. It was natural for our father to teach us to fly fish and to shoot. We both learned to shoot on a double-barrelled 410 hammer gun which had belonged to our grandfather La Touche. Shooting around us mainly consisted of snipe with the odd pheasant, duck, woodcock or partridge. Michael and I spent much of our winter holidays stalking green plover in the fields up near Lynch's Cross with some success but I don't think my father approved of this activity. My father also disapproved of shooting hares and the big disincentive was that you had to carry the animal home with you which could be some distance if you were out on a long shoot. One day the three of us went out shooting snipe in a rushy field just off the Kells road. Some snipe got up and we all fired off our guns. Michael started to jeer our father for having shot a hare which he had seen fall over when our father had fired his gun. Our father got extremely annoyed and marched forward to pick up the snipe which he had shot. The unfortunate hare had been hit by a stray pellet. Michael really loved his game and ate the brains of the birds. He also ate all kinds of offal—my mother really enjoyed cooking for him. Other than shooting during the winter another activity was ice skating when it was cold enough to freeze some of the local ponds. Michael took particular pleasure in these traditions and even when he married Barbara and moved away he would ring our father to find out if skating was feasible. When Michael and I lived in Montreal we skated on a regular basis on the local ice rink so we had become quite proficient on the blades. I can still picture Michael hurtling around Leavy's pond near Kilskyre with the thin ice cracking and waving up and down.

There are always things about Michael in Johnsbrook that I can still clearly see and often have dreams about. Frequently these are associated with being in the basement where he had a collection of vintage wines. When Michael was in UCD he sold wine, mainly 1952 and '53 clarets and burgundys, for a cousin of ours, who named his company 'Vintage Wines'. The company went out of business sometime in the 1960s and the wine was put in storage. In the late 1960s Michael saw an ad in the paper for the sale of this wine which he bought and stored in the basement of Johnsbrook. He then set up a small wholesale company which he called 'Rare Wines'. After I returned from Canada in order to go to college, Michael asked me if I would help him with the small wine concern. He made all the contacts and bought new wine at auctions and other small wholesalers. I looked after the sales, deliveries etc.

One day every weekend Michael would come down from Dublin to Johnsbrook to work in his ten-acre fruit farm which he had purchased from our father. Every Saturday evening I would take out a couple of vintage bottles for sampling in the dining room prior to dinner. This became a weekly ritual. One Saturday evening I arrived up to the dining room with two bottles for sampling and I noticed a young man sitting in the corner and assumed he was one of Margaret's (our youngest sister) friends. I was very rude and ignored him or just grunted at him since there was more serious business at hand. Then Michael came in and walked over to the table where I had decanted the wine for tasting. Michael said to me 'Who is your man?' and I said 'I don't know' and the two of us tasted the wine and having found it satisfactory left the room.

This was our first sighting of James Nugent (now SC) who married Margaret. Michael read widely about wines and was very shrewd in what he purchased but the main thing was that it gave memorable drinking evenings in Johnsbrook with a fine roast put on the table by our mother. My other strong memory of Michael was to see him sitting at the end of the dinning room with his polo neck sweater and policeman's jacket tucking into a mound of Spanish rice (rice cooked with home-grown tomatoes and spiced-up) with sweat pouring off his forehead. Michael's theory for beating the heat was to wear as many clothes as possible to keep the heat out.

These are just my own memories of Michael while we were in Johnsbrook, but all of us siblings found great support from him. When I came back from Canada and while at college, I stayed some time with him and Barbara for which I have always been grateful. It was he who encouraged me to take up archaeology and drop economics, which turned out to be a very wise move. There are lots of other things I could write about like fishing in Donegal and the endless pulling of the curragh for mackerel, walking on long treks up hills and bogs to go trout fishing with our father. Michael was the rock of strength and sense on which our family stood and I will always miss him and still dream about him.

A journey interrupted

Denis Corboy*

Michael was my closest school friend at Glenstal and subsequently at UCD. Our association began through the school magazine, which Michael edited and for which I was the ill informed and over enthusiastic, fairly hopeless music critic. The Sweetman association with the Benedictines went back a long way. The first Benedictine school in Ireland, Mount Saint Benedict, had been opened at Gorey in 1905–6. Dom John Francis Sweetman was one of its founders and ran the school until it closed in 1925. Mount Saint Benedict influenced a generation of middle-class Catholic Irishmen, who, it must be said, were mostly of the Cumann na nGaedheal/Fine Gael persuasion.

The Gorey ethos of a liberal education based on the classics was carried through to Glenstal under the influence of Dom Matthew Dillon, who was our headmaster during the early years. Father Matthew, who had an Irish Party political pedigree—youngest son of John Dillon MP and brother of James Dillon—was a formidable personality who never compromised his anti-republicanism and constitutional approach to Irish nationalism.

The Sweetman political DNA, with its roots in Irish politics, was contagious. Even though we were confined in a monastic boarding school, we were avid daily readers of *The Irish Times*, seen outside as liberal and Protestant, of course the *Indo*, and the monthly journal of Irish liberal opinion *The Leader*. Our conversation and the school debates invariably focused on the kind of Ireland we looked forward to and we were always in search of a new narrative. We saw ourselves as being way to the left of the traditional politics of the day. As precocious socialistically minded school kids we became fascinated by the

* Denis Corboy was a founder member of the European Movement in Ireland. He headed the European Commission in Ireland for nine years before being posted to Washington. He is the Director of the Caucasus Policy Institute of King's College, London.

new thinking coming from mainland Europe. The country had just taken its first steps in joining the Council of Europe and the inspiration of the Schuman Declaration and Jean Monnet's Coal and Steel Community seemed to provide the narrative that we were looking for. A European future for Ireland became a lively subject of debate long before we left boarding school in 1954.

At a very early stage Michael and I took a keen interest in good wine. Secretly we formed a wine club, against all the rules of the school, of course, which met under cover of night in the woods. More than one monk from the monastery was a regular attendee. This interest in wine continued.

Both Michael and I went to UCD and took the same degree course known as VIIIB History. The History Department, led by Professors Dudley Edwards and Desmond Williams, and lecturers such as Kevin B. Nowlan and Hugh Kearney, had the reputation for being the best for historical studies in Ireland. We were very fortunate to be exposed to new intellectual challenges and above all being taught to question traditional and received truth, not least the mythologies which informed Irish nationalism.

Apart from broadening one's understanding of the world, there was also a fun side to university life. I was billeted in Hatch Street and my room overlooked the backyard of the Sacred Heart Convent in Leeson Street. One of the innocent pastimes was to watch the senior girls on their bicycles coming and going. Our star was a very beautiful, tall, elegant blonde girl and after some research we learnt both her name and that she would be coming to UCD the following September. We discovered also that one of our close friends knew her sister Rosemary and as soon as we returned after the summer holidays we set about finding an opportunity to meet. A regular haunt at weekends was 'the hop' at the Incorporated Law Society. I asked my good friend to invite Rosemary and suggest that her sister should also come along.

All worked according to plan and the evening was a great success. Rosemary's sister turned out to be Barbara Becker from Palmerston Road. I reported on these events to the usual group of ex-school friends who met nightly in O'Dwyer's pub at the bottom of Leeson Street. We called ourselves the Scoop Club and the other members, including Michael, had also met Barbara at college. The discussion led to a bet that the first person among us to ask her for a date would be stood a pint by each of the rest. The conversation moved on to other things and Michael seemed to disappear but within minutes he returned to announce that he had set up a date with Barbara for the following day. Celebrations were in order and all the debts were immediately paid in full. The rest, as they say, is history. Their student romance led to early marriage, great happiness and a charming and successful Sweetman-size family.

After graduation and marriage in 1957, Michael and Barbara went to live in Canada. When they returned to Dublin in the mid-1960s, he joined the Federation of Irish Industries, the predecessor of the Confederation of Irish Industry, as director of information, later becoming director of business policy.

In the meantime, I had gone to the Law Library and started practice as a barrister. In our student days, we had all been involved with the European Youth Campaign (EYC) run by the great Miriam Hederman O'Brien. The EYC was the youth branch of the European Movement and through its meetings and conferences we became committed to the belief that Ireland's future destiny was as part of the European project. From the early 1960s onwards I was combining practice at the Bar, the Munster Circuit and honorary director of the Irish Council of the European Movement. I added a further complication to this in 1963 by accepting a contract from the European Commission to be their Irish adviser which eventually led to the opening of the Commission's Information Office in Dublin in 1968. Things were moving at a pace but were brought to a sudden halt by General de Gaulle's second veto on membership later that year. My Commissioner at the time, Albert Coppe, supported the idea that, rather than staying around, I should take up an Eisenhower fellowship and go to the United States for six months. When I returned to Dublin it became clear that being the Commission man could not be combined with directing the local European Movement, and furthermore EEC membership negotiations appeared almost certainly on the cards.

When Michael came back from Canada he immediately took a leading part in the European Movement and became a prominent spokesman and debater. With the prospect of a referendum on membership looming he was the obvious person to lead the campaign as its director. It took us no small degree of persuasion for the FII to second him for this purpose. I think he played the critical role in preparing public opinion and in articulating the pro case prior to and during the 1972 referendum.

When I look back on those years, the qualities I always remember about Michael were his clarity of thought, integrity and courage of conviction. I greatly admired his ability with words and his lucid fluid writing style. I have met very few people in my life with such a gift. He led a remarkable and brilliant campaign which helped turn a new and exciting page in Irish history.

The world we had imagined and dreamt about for so many years was suddenly and inexplicably ended by the Staines disaster. I still believe that all twelve who died that day would have played key influential roles in the future of Ireland and also the future of the new Europe. In so many ways, I believe things would not have been the same if this tragedy had not occurred. Michael had all the qualities and talent to become an inspiring future leader of Fine Gael and leader of the country. Whenever I consider what is happening in Ireland today and the constant crises in European integration and the eurozone I ask myself 'what would Michael have said and done?' Most certainly he would have been at the heart of the current debate and a strong voice of reason and wisdom. We are all the losers for his absence.

Golden days

Caroline Stephenson

One of the things I loved about my father was that he could change from being a smart businessman during the week and on Saturdays look like a tramp.

Saturdays were Johnsbrook days as my father donned his old britches and jacket to go to work on his fruit farm in Co. Meath. My twin Michèle and I would go with him on alternative Saturdays, and then the following week our other siblings, Patrick, Christopher, Rachel, Tim.

En route we would stop in Trim to buy meat from a butcher there, to bring home to Dublin for the week. The fruit farm called Beggars Bush, of about 10 acres, was on land bought from his parents and located just up the road from their home, Johnsbrook.

My father would spend the day working on the fruit farm and Michèle and I would spend the day with Granny. Memories of happy hours spent chatting with her, sitting by the fireplace in the dining-room at Johnsbrook, or going into Carrolls in Kells, shopping. Granny had a calm, unconditional quality of love and I loved to be with her. She adored my father and they had a special bond. Almost to the day, a year after he was killed, she suffered a stroke and died a few months later.

Johnsbrook, of course, also meant Pop. A great character with a sharp sense of humour. The sheriff of Trim, as he told us children, or more commonly known as the County Registrar! He had a wonderful bold grin and while sometimes gruff and scary, to me anyway, his bark was much worse than his bite! Together with Granny, he created the wonderful atmosphere of Johnsbrook.

Saturday nights at Johnsbrook would be a festive coming together of whoever was around for a delicious dinner cooked by Granny. It always seemed to have a great sense of occasion. My father had bought wines from a cousin of his who had been a wine merchant. He now sold them through a company called Vintage Wines, a sideline with his brother David. On Saturday nights there was always great ceremony in decanting and sampling some of the stock. Michèle and I would sit shyly at the table absorbing the lively discussions on politics, family lore and general animated conversation.

I adored my father. I idolised him with my childish eyes up to the day he died. I thought then that perhaps I had this idealistic childish version of him because he died while I was still so young, aged fourteen. But talking to Donal Flynn for this book made me realise that it was not mere childish admiration for he described so well the man I remember. The irreverence yet great charm, the energy and the impatience with artifice. The sense of humour and the integrity of the man. When I think of my father I remember a person I felt safe with, a person I felt was on my side, who was full of ideas and enthusiasm for life, always ready to embrace the new and always up to something.

It seemed he was bursting at the seams of our suburban house in Foxrock, making cider, beer, wine, collecting stamps, electioneering, canvassing, the classical music on Sunday mornings blasting through the house, the teases, the jokes, a man bubbling over with life and energy.

I remember him saying that one day people would be going to the moon for their holidays.

In Donegal, where his parents had a holiday home, still there, I remember Daddy tying a blanket to his shoulders and jumping off a sand dune trying to be Batman! And always of course on the hottest days on the beach wearing an Aran jumper and woollen jacket, maintaining it kept the heat off.

The wonderful fishing trips with Pop, Uncle Hugh, David and the rest of us, trudging across bogs to get to that special lake, full of fish! The picnics complete with the volcanic kettle to make tea, a day's expedition. Collecting mussels and Daddy scrubbing off the barnacles outside the back door before making a delicious sauce to cook them in. Daddy telling Michèle and me to wear the wrong coloured socks so that we would be sent home from school and he would have an excuse to take us out. His aunt was a nun in the school. My father being the only uncool adult to wear a lifejacket when we went on a cruising trip on the Shannon. And of course he was vindicated as an adult did fall in, but thankfully came out unharmed. Then in the last years before he was killed, I remember going to meetings with him and being so proud listening to him talk and loving the way he would introduce us as his daughters.

To remember my father is also to remember my mother. They are both an integral part of my very happy childhood. They were such a team. I have no memories of ever hearing a cross word between them, only the very strong sense of their love and joy in each other and their shared endeavour.

I remember being so proud of them both dressed up to go out, such a beautiful couple. My mother's laughter ringing through the house when they were having a dinner party and I was upstairs in bed. A lovely sound to go to sleep to! My mother's singing and her dancing and the sense of my father's pride in her. And always the sound of their laughter.

We were a lucky, happy bunch! Boisterous, the wooden spoon became a feature at the dinner table and it was used. But it was not wounding and the laughter went on.

And then the day the laughter stopped. The day my father was killed. I shall never forget the look on my mother's face on the day of the funeral. The dream had died.

Behind the scenes: Michael's contributions to Fine Gael policy formulation

John Dillon*

My memories of my cousin Michael go back a long way, in fact to the autumn of 1946, when my part of the family returned from the mid-West of the United States, and settled down on the next estate to the Sweetman domain of Johnsbrook, Triermore, in the depths of Co. Meath. Our mothers were sisters, Mary (Mimi) and Elizabeth (Bessie) La Touche, and they resumed a close cooperation which had been interrupted by years of separation—since my parents had headed off for Madison, Wisconsin, back in 1937.

Johnsbrook in particular was something of a paradise for small persons, with meadows, lakes and woods (enriched with tree-houses and 'dens'), and a large rambling house with yard and walled garden. We ran an 'empire', presided over benignly by Michael, as the senior member—I seem to remember even producing our own coins and stamps!—which tended rather to strike terror into neighbouring children when they came over for birthday parties and the like. But Johnsbrook was a popular venue, nonetheless.

Looking back on it, I was undoubtedly something of an oddity—awkward, overweight, with a strong mid-Western American accent, and something of a stutter, but I don't remember being made anything but welcome by Michael. Indeed, when in the summer of 1948 I proceeded, following him and David, to St Gerard's School, Bray,

* John Dillon retired in 2006 as Regius Professor of Greek in Trinity College Dublin. Born in 1939 in Madison, Wisconsin, USA, he returned to Ireland in 1945, attended the same preparatory school as Michael (St Gerard's, Bray), before returning in 1966 to the USA to pursue graduate work in the University of California in Berkeley, where he joined the Classics faculty in 1969, returning to take up the Chair of Greek in Trinity in 1980

I recall him drawing me aside on my first day and delivering certain avuncular warnings as to how to behave and what to watch out for. The only piece of advice that I remember was on no account to reveal to anyone the names of one's sisters. But there were certainly others. He may also have warned me against asking for 'Lil Bars' at the school tuckshop, presided over by our headmaster's wife, known as Ma Lil. New boys were persuaded that 'Lil Bars' were a particular delicacy of the house, and they were by all means to request them. Why the schoolboy mind found this so hilarious is now quite beyond me to conjecture, but we did.

My parents moved down to the vicinity of Dublin, in fact, later in 1948, since my father was now attached to the Dublin Institute of Advanced Studies (he had previously been away in Edinburgh), and I would have had much less to do with my senior cousin until he came for a while to board with us, in the mid-1950s, when he was attending UCD. I had by that time gone on to Downside, in Somerset, so that I was away most of the time. All I remember of Michael then was a deeply laid-back figure, whom my mother had considerable difficulty in getting out of bed to attend his lectures. At any rate, this did not prevent him from getting a perfectly respectable degree in History in the summer of 1956. And after that he and Barbara went off to Canada, until 1963.

Really, then, my only meaningful interaction with Michael on an adult level came in the mid-1960s, from 1963 to 1966, when he had returned from Montreal, and was with the Confederation of Irish Industry, but had also become actively involved with the most forward-looking aspects of Fine Gael, namely the Central Branch, and its journal *The Citizen*, with which I was also concerned. That was an exciting time, the era of the Just Society, when it seemed for a while that it might be possible to interest the dear old party (then led by my Uncle James) in something approaching 'ideas'.

As for myself, having graduated from Oxford in 1961, I headed off to Ethiopia to teach English and goof off generally, while brooding much, in a juvenile sort of way, on the Meaning of Life and the Future of Western Civilisation, and dabbling in fiction of various kinds. I returned to Dublin, like Michael, in 1963, and embarked first on a law degree in UCD and the King's Inns, with the vague idea of going into politics, or perhaps becoming a writer, or both. However, after a year of taking lectures in UCD from such luminaries as John Kelly and John Blayney, and eating dinners in the King's Inns, I turned back to an interest in things academic, and specifically Ancient Philosophy, and this involved taking a job teaching Classics in Glenstal in the autumn of 1964, while starting a Ph. D. under John O'Meara in UCD. This in turn involved living in Limerick, in a flat in Pery Square, with my new wife Jean, and involvement in the social and political life of Limerick, which in fact turned out to be quite lively, though largely of an 'underground' nature, viewed with general hostility by the Confraternity of the Holy Family, which still dominated public life.

So Michael was in Dublin and I was now in Limerick, reducing interaction once again to a minimum, despite my continued involvement in grassroots politics, through the local branch of the Fine Gael Youth Group, of which I was chairman. In Dublin, Michael had become actively involved with the Central Branch (to which I think I may have introduced him), and in contributing to *The Citizen*, and in November 1965 he was invited by Liam Cosgrave, who had taken over as leader in the wake of the general election from my Uncle James, to be a member of the National Council of Fine Gael, a testament to the growing regard in which he was held.

The Presidential Campaign of 1966

I was not much in touch with Michael, I think, during 1965. However, the Presidential campaign of Tom O'Higgins in the spring of 1966 produced a welcome development in our relations, since Michael, who was by now a valued advisor and speech-writer for the Fine Gael party, particularly on agricultural and EEC-related topics, was called upon to assist Tom O'Higgins in enunciating some forward-looking ideas, and in that connection he called me onto his team.

The operation began with an invitation from Liam Cosgrave (by letter of 4 March 1966) to Michael to join a team consisting of Garret FitzGerald, Alexis FitzGerald, Tom Finlay, Patrick Dillon-Malone, and Declan Costello, to construct suitable scripts for the O'Higgins campaign. This group were to meet—and presumably did meet—the following Tuesday, 8 March. The call for scripts followed in a note dated 18 April, and everyone got to work.

This is not by any means to suggest that O'Higgins himself was devoid of ideas. In fact, there is attached to this later note of 18 April a memo from Tom, listing a number of his primary concerns, on which scripts might be composed. He is concerned with defining a new nationalism, which will embrace all inhabitants of Northern Ireland in an Ireland to which they could grant allegiance; a concern with our ideal level of population and its employment; a concern with proper norms of social justice in respect of health care and education; and an exploration of our relations with the rest of Europe. All these were issues on which Michael had strong views, but he was plainly not alone in this. Nonetheless, it is possible from the papers to recover some sense of his contribution.

I include here two documents which seem to me to reflect rather well Michael's thinking at this time on a number of issues, all of which surfaced in the course of the campaign. One is a sort of position paper, which may have served as a press release; the other an extract from a speech. First, the 'position paper':

The President of Ireland should represent in his own person the highest ideals of the Irish people. He is uniquely placed to set a tone for the whole nation. He is above politics and has no political power, and cannot therefore lead the nation on specific issues as a Taoiseach does. Yet his influence could be considerable. A man of real stature as President could be a constant source of inspiration by demonstrating in his own attitudes and activities those virtues and ideals which we put before ourselves as a nation.

In a recent speech, the Taoiseach admitted that, contrary to what he himself had in the past suggested, those who followed John Redmond in 1914 and went to fight in France, 'did so from the highest motives.' Nothing could be clearer evidence of the fact that most Irish people are turning away in disgust from the narrow-minded and bigoted attitudes toward other political views which have been the stock-in-trade of Mr Lemass's party for the last forty years. Instead, people want a broader kind of patriotic ideal—a patriotism big enough to include all Irishmen who love their country, even if they do not agree with 1916, or Sinn Féin, or the revival of the Irish language.

The man we elect as President can play a key role in encouraging this larger, more generous patriotism which belongs to the new, young Ireland emerging today. Only this kind of outlook can lead to a reconciliation with our fellow-countrymen in the North. The man Fine Gael have nominated for President is this kind of person—young, forward-looking, generous and broadminded. His election would symbolise dramatically our progress towards the kind of Irish nation fought for in 1916—an Irish nation that could include the whole of Ireland, united not only geographically, but in heart and mind.

Second, some extracts from the speech, the whole of which is a very interesting historical meditation on how we got to where we are (or were in 1966), and how we could move on from there:

> This country is, at the moment, in a kind of ideological vacuum. Over the past few years, the ideals which largely dominated Irish politics since the foundation of the State have faded away. They have become discredited because people realised increasingly that political leaders kept talking about them as a cover-up for doing nothing about some of the extremely urgent practical problems which faced the country. So, in little more than a decade, we have thrown out the notion that nothing matters so long as the Irish nation is separated in every possible way from England, and have replaced it with an attitude—one cannot call it an ideology—that economic progress is the only thing that matters. In other words, let's get rich quick, and never mind how we do it.
>
> One very immediate example of this attitude is the way in which we are allowing the whole centre of our capital city to be transformed not according to any positive programme, generally approved by the community: instead by property speculators whose only concern is to get maximum financial return for themselves from the piece of property which they own. In the same way, we have allowed the open country all around the city to be bought up by speculative builders and covered with big blocks of housing of very doubtful aesthetic value. We have, thus, thrown away for ever a unique opportunity.

All this, of course, sounds remarkably prescient in view of the events of the last decade, but those of us who were around at the time can recall that it was an accurate evaluation of what was happening then. This was, however, for Michael just an introduction to his main theme, which was the current loss of national purpose, and the search for such a purpose for the future.

In this connection, he surveys most areas of national life, but particularly our failures in the areas of education and agriculture. He argues against the ideology of separatism and an exclusively Gaelic identity, and ends as follows:

> What then should be our attitude for the future? Firstly, we must frankly recognise that even if Ireland ever was a purely Gaelic nation, nearly a

thousand years of history have totally transformed it, so that it has as little relevance to present-day Ireland as Queen Boadicea's Celtic kingdom has to Britain. The Gaelic strands in our heritage are woven with the Norman, the English, the Scandinavian, the Scottish, the Continental,[1] blended in so completely that we cannot pull them out without destroying the whole cloth, and leaving ourselves with a tattered piece of rag. Ireland is a country moulded and shaped over the centuries by all these influences. The Irish nation draws a vital facet of its personality from each of them. The unique experience of being Irish is to share in the whole of this rich heritage.

We must learn to recognise that the Orangeman of the North is as truly Irish as we are, that he is no less Irish because his political views differ from ours. We must abandon definitions of nationality and patriotism which exclude a large number of our fellow-countrymen, because only then can we hope for an Ireland united in heart and mind, as well as geographically. Only by reawakening this concept of an Irish nation can we rediscover the sense of national purpose which alone can give meaning to our independence and to our future. This is an ideal which would make us worthy of the long generations of our past, an ideal which would justify our long struggle to establish and preserve our national identity, an ideal which would give us a nation that we in turn can be proud to pass on to our children, and to the generations of the future.

A good deal of this did find its way into the speeches of the candidate during the course of the campaign, which ran from mid-April to the end of May. I recall in that connection having considerable fun in trying to get daring notions and turns of phrase past the censorship (we were not, for instance, allowed to attack Dev, or indeed to refer to him in any way—probably a good idea, on reflection), and, despite the best efforts of Comdt. Sanfey and the Central Office, Tom O'Higgins did end up saying some interesting things, and certainly giving old Dev a bit of a fright, even if victory was probably out of the question, without a Brian Lenihan-style faux pas, such as was not vouchsafed to us. Still, to get within 20,000 votes of the old cod, in an electorate of just over 1,000,000, was not at all bad, and Michael certainly played a significant part in that.[2]

---

1 He himself, of course, being a combination of Scandinavian Sweetmans and Huguenot La Touches.

2 In fact, percentage-wise, Dev won by just 50.48 per cent to 49.52 per cent—pretty much of a whisker. Tom O'Higgins, it may be noted, won in all the Dublin con-

Michael as political adviser, 1965–72

Jean and I left for Berkeley, California, shortly after the election, in the autumn of 1966, but Michael went on to become a major force behind the scenes in the party, particularly, as I say, in the area of agriculture, where he provided forceful copy for the spokesman on agriculture, Mark Clinton, over the next few years. I find, for instance, in Michael's papers, the following hard-hitting indictment of the Fianna Fáil government dated 14 March 1969, in the run-up to the general election of that spring:

> It is obvious that the present government has decided to write off the agricultural industry. This is very clearly revealed in the part of the so-called Third Programme dealing with agriculture. This document makes it perfectly clear that the present government sees little future for Irish agriculture. Apparently it believes that nothing more is needed in an agricultural policy for the 1970s than for the Department of Agriculture to grind along in the same old way with the same policies or lack of policies which are responsible for the very serious problems which face the Irish farmer today. While the present government can see all the problems which provide it with an excuse for doing nothing, it seems unable to recognise the opportunities—for example, our really favourable conditions for low cost, high output, meat production.

He goes on to outline Fine Gael's proposals for involving farmers much more actively in planning for development, and thus increasing their confidence in the efficacy of government policies, and setting up a Rural Development Authority, with strong farmer participation, which would report directly to the Minister. Above all, drawing on his expertise within the Confederation of Irish Industry, he calls for a radical improvement in marketing:

> Sound marketing strategies can only be developed if the approximate quantities of each commodity which will be available for market are known. If proper planning and marketing techniques are used, targets can be set, steps can be taken to build up production, and at the same time plans can be laid for orderly marketing of that production. Without planning of this kind, we are going to have constant repetition of the situation which has occurred constantly under Fianna Fáil governments—production being encouraged without proper market planning, followed by collapse of markets and severe losses to farmers.

stituencies, and three out of the four Cork ones.

Indeed, two and a half years previously, in an article in *The Citizen* in September 1966, he had excoriated Minister for Agriculture Charles Haughey, in the wake of his new Trade Agreement with Britain, for encouraging Irish farmers to increase beef production without taking any thought as to the marketing of this beef, with the result that the bottom fell out of the market, leaving many of them at considerable loss. He calls there for the setting up of a Meat Marketing Board, 'to ensure that increased production would not simply result, as in the past, in collapsing markets.' Running through all his thinking in these years is in fact the concern, derived from his expertise in the area of marketing, for the long-term planning of Irish agricultural production.

Moving forward some years, to the run-up to the Fine Gael Árd Fheis of May 1968, we find in the papers a significant sequence of documents, showing how central Michael had become to policy-making for the party by this time. First, there is a letter from Liam Cosgrave dated 26 April, acknowledging the importance of Michael's previous contributions, and asking for a script that he can deliver to the Árd Fheis. It is worth quoting, I think, at some length, as it shows the full sweep of Michael's interests:

Dear Michael,

A propos of our conversation on the telephone, I telephoned today but learned you had gone to Killarney.[3] In case I do not see you before I go,[4] I thought it as well to put some items on paper concerning the Árd Fheis speech.

At this stage it seems to me that it would be appropriate to give a broad general outline of Fine Gael policy, setting out all that has been done, and putting it forward in general terms as the Fine Gael plan for the 70s.

This might be sketched under broad headings: economic, educational, health and social policy, local government and industrial relations. These are not put in any order, but just mentioned as they appear. In respect of industry and agriculture, I thought you might set out our plan incorporating the general recommendations in respect of industry, including in it the Federation of Irish Industries pamphlet *Challenger* which we spoke about the other day, and also the industrial relations on the lines of the

3 Presumably for the annual meeting of the Federation of Irish Industries (predecessor to the CII).

4 Cosgrave was off to New York, to fulfil some speaking engagements.

script you did for the meeting in the Television Club which, as you know, I used in full.[5] Unless there is a concerted effort by all concerned in industry to provide a set framework for solving industrial relations, economic progress will be hindered.

In respect of agriculture, two big problems that seem difficult of solution are the extent to which subsidies have to be provided for milk and pigs, which has resulted up to the present in respect of milk in a huge surplus for which it is difficult to find markets. Is marketing the problem or should production be diverted to other lines?

I suppose the speech should also have some general criticism of the failure of the Second Programme.

Michael duly obliged, with a speech that attracted the malevolent attention of John Healy, writing as 'Backbencher' in *The Irish Times* of Saturday 18 May. One cannot be quite sure how much Cosgrave may have contributed to the speech himself, but Healy plainly thought not much. He discerns the sinister influence of Michael Sweetman throughout, but especially in a passage which commends the views of Sicco Mansfeld, the then EEC Commissioner for Agriculture, on the future of European agriculture, and the desirability of encouraging farm units of an economically useful size, a proposal which Healy, as a defender of the 'old ways', views with abhorrence:

> I wish Mr Cosgrave was more familiar with his script. I am understanding enough: my charity is virtually inexhaustible, and I know he was just back from New York and in a mood which did not predispose him to being cool, calm and collected. But if he must use a speechwriter or two, I do wish he'd think out where the words will end up and how they will be read.
>
> Nor do I resent Mr Michael Sweetman's right to shape Irish society as he sees fit. Mr Michael Sweetman is one of the 'think-tank' people in Fine Gael. He is closely associated with the National Industrial and Economic Council—the NIEC. He wrote *Challenge*, which is the lobby publication of the Federation of Irish Industries. The NIEC, to repeat the much-quoted words of My Senior Assistant among others, is noted for one thing: it has not on its council a single agriculturalist. It, nevertheless, felt itself capable of predicting the future shape of Ireland and Irish society into the 1980s with its blueprint for full employment. That blueprint called for the extermination of thousands of people now living on the

5 This was a speech to Fine Gael supporters within the trade union movement, delivered on 9 March, of which a script exists in the papers. It is a most interesting document.

land which, according to the NIEC slide-rule whizkids, would flee it for an urban life.

Mr Sweetman is a subscriber to that decision.

This week Mr Cosgrave became a subscriber to the Sweetman doctrine.

Of course, Healy had a very particular agenda: the defence of the small farmer, and the traditional life-style of the West of Ireland, so we must expect something of a rant here. In fact, what was particularly annoying him was Michael's relaying of Mansfeld's judgment that 'the smallest dairy farm unit which would be economical in Europe in the future would be one including about 400 cows, and keeping five men fully employed.' 'That,' Michael wrote for Liam Cosgrave, 'is a statement to which one ought to give serious thought. It is clearly ludicrous to base our dairy policy in Ireland on the small one-man farm, if, five or ten years from now, these are not going to have any chance of survival.'

Now this is in one way the merest common sense, but it would also signal the demise of the great majority of farms in Ireland, and the destruction of a way of life. This naturally roused Healy's ire, but he is quite unjustified in suggesting that Michael was not an agriculturalist (whatever precisely that is supposed to be). Michael, as we know, had thought long and deeply about the position of Irish agriculture, and he did in fact maintain during all this time a fruit farm of his own near his ancestral homestead in Co. Meath, which I can remember visiting, and on which all the family had to join in the tillage and harvesting. Michael's concern, in contrast to Healy, was simply the survival of agriculture as a viable industry in a larger European context, such as he was anticipating Ireland joining in the next few years. As he writes for Liam Cosgrave:

> In five or ten years' time no man in his senses is going to be prepared to work seven days a week, three hundred and sixty-five days in the year, for an income of £300, or £500, or £700, or even £1000, a year. Yet our present agricultural policies seem to assume that they will; but again to quote Mr. Mansholt, 'What is important is not the family farm, but the farm family'.

That, as he goes on to specify, excludes the small, one-man farm from consideration as an economic entity.

The speech goes on to make very sound proposals in the area of industrial development, industrial relations, health and social welfare, but our chief focus in this segment of my essay is on agriculture. In this area my Uncle James would have been, I think, very much of the same mind as John Healy, but I fear that from a practical point of view he would have been equally wrong; Michael saw clearly what had to be done to place Irish agriculture on a firm footing for the future, and he enunciated it again and again in the years leading up to his untimely death.

In conclusion, one can only lament, first of all, that in the two general elections of 1965 and 1969, where Michael would have had a significant influence on policy had Fine Gael attained power, the obstinacy and misguided optimism of the Labour Party under Brendan Corish precluded any pre-election coalition pact, and thus allowed first Lemass and then Jack Lynch to scrape back in, and then that the tragic plane crash of 18 June 1972 preceded Fine Gael's ultimate accession to power in February 1973.

But so life goes.

An appreciation

Liam Cosgrave*

I was fortunate to have Michael Sweetman as an adviser when he worked in a voluntary capacity while I was party leader. At that time the party could not afford to pay for professional political advice and he worked regularly without any remuneration.

His advice on a variety of matters was most useful, in particular when drafting speeches. His knowledge of economic affairs was considerable especially in farming interests. He had a realistic and practical view on the nation's economy. He enjoyed writing scripts in which he had a remarkable output and if sometimes I did not use what he had written he would say quietly, 'I expected that'.

Michael was always most courteous and easy to work with and showed the same consideration to all those involved in such activity. Usually the help he gave me was after he had already completed a day's work—a clear example of his total commitment to what he believed in and his dedication to the public interest. He served without remuneration to the full extent of his remarkable ability.

It is for me a real pleasure to express my appreciation of the work he did in which he showed such accomplishment in the written word.

* Liam Cosgrave was a TD from 1943 to 1981, and became Parliamentary Secretary to Taoiseach John A.Costello in 1948. He was Leader of Fine Gael from 1965 to 1977 and Taoiseach from 1973 to 1977.

A remarkable man

Garret FitzGerald*

Michael Sweetman was one of the most remarkable people I have met. He came of a family which had played a part in Irish politics at least since Parnell's time, and in the 1960s an older cousin of his, Gerard Sweetman, was deputy leader of Fine Gael, until killed in a tragic car accident in 1970.

Despite the fact that Michael and Gerard were both involved in Fine Gael at the same time, they were politically poles apart. Gerard, a solicitor, was a pragmatic, conservative, business-oriented, down-to-earth politician. Michael was emphatically on the left—a liberal intellectual and above all an ideas-man. I met him in the mid-1960s at a conference in Copenhagen, when I was chairman of the Hosiery and Knitwear Adaptation Council and he was working for our export board, Córas Tráchtála. Initially I was misled by his deceptively languid manner and mode of speech. But in the years that followed he and Barbara became close friends of Joan and myself.

I was attracted by his markedly original mind, unselfconscious lack of respect for convention, and mischievous sense of humour. He had a delightful lack of respect for the many sacred cows that then littered the Irish political landscape. And when he became Tom O'Higgins's speech-writer during the Presidential election campaign of 1966, I came to realise that he was a highly skilful and strongly committed political figure.

In that campaign Tom, then in his late forties and with a young family, represented an emerging second generation, on whose behalf he was challenging de Valera's uni-cultural view of Ireland. He espoused an open multi-culturalism which, for the first time in Irish

* Garret FitzGerald (1926-2011) was Minister for Foreign Affairs from 1973 to 1977, was twice Taoiseach, from June 1981 to March 1982 and from December 1982 to March 1987. Chancellor of the National University of Ireland from 1997 to 2007, he was a columnist for *The Irish Times* from 1954 to 2011.

politics was including Northern unionism as an essential strand of Irish society.

Michael was deeply committed to this pluralist approach, and gave voice to it in brilliant speeches he drafted for the candidate, which soon struck a welcome note with many of those who had grown up in Ireland since independence. When combined with Peter Prendergast's remarkable organisation of the whole O'Higgins electoral campaign, this swung much of public opinion.

However, in the absence of opinion polls, (which played no role in politics until the late 1970s), very few people believed that de Valera was close to being defeated—until the votes were counted, when the outgoing President was found to have won by a margin of only 1 per cent!

From then on until Michael's tragic death in the Staines air disaster in 1972 he and I became political allies, and close friends. He shared my deep commitment to finding a solution that would end the violence in Northern Ireland, and twice accompanied Tom O'Higgins and myself to Northern Ireland: first to meet John Hume in late 1969, and again to the shattering funeral of the victims of the British paratroopers in Derry in early 1972.

The late 1960s and early 1970s was a difficult time for me in Fine Gael, because of divisions in the party. Throughout those years I found Michael a tower of strength and naturally looked forward to a future in which over many years we would work together to transform our country.

The Staines disaster cost Ireland much of its future business leadership. But it also deprived us of one of the most original Irish political thinkers of the late twentieth century.

Ode for my father

Michèle Sweetman

From collar studs, cufflinks, three piece suit
To Aran jumper, lumber jacket and policeman's britches
From the office and political affairs
To the fruit farm, collecting bags of soot along the way
Daddy on television, Daddy on his farm

Daddy fishing with Pop, David and Uncle Hugh
'Be the holy you've got one, throw it back it's just a shrew!'
Donegal picnics, volcano kettle, sardine sandwiches, thigh-high
        wader boots, 'whoopee'
Jumping from a sand dune: rug as cloak Batman swoops!

Sunday afternoons sacrosanct, you and BB reading the papers.
Bach, Handel or Beethoven full blast.
Children do not interfere.
There's Tortoise and Snail and me the Slug and Kipper
and Moppit and Timmit the babe.

Saturday mornings and off to Johnsbrook!
You took two of us with you to join in the fest
Granny in the dairy separating the cream
'Don't tell your grandmother how to suck eggs' her favourite refrain.
All day running and having a ball
Playing in the vintage car you kept in the yard
As blissful a childhood as any could dream of.

By evening the work was done out of doors
Indoors the log fires roaring, table set, cellar visited, vintage wine de-
canted, breathing. Granny's feast coming up in the lift! Pop at the top
of the table, Granny by his side. You at the other end giving it lip.
Us in the middle quiet as mice basking in the glory of your reflected
        light.
Heading back in the dark of night, TK lemonade in Athboy

And then you took flight . . .

Michael Sweetman and the Confederation of Irish Industry

Liam Connellan*

Michael Sweetman joined the staff of the Federation of Irish Industries (FII) in 1964 as Director of Information. As Director of Business Policy at what had by then become the Confederation of Irish Industry, he was seconded in 1971 to assume the role of Director of the Irish Council of the European Movement to lead the campaign in favour of Ireland's entry to the EEC. This chapter highlights his influence within these organisations particularly in the crucial years prior to the vote in favour of membership of the EEC, and also the key economic issues facing industry in Ireland in the years before and after membership of the EEC.

The FII was established in 1932 to represent the interests of manufacturing industry to all levels of government, initially to ensure that tariff protection was effective.

In the early 1930s tariff protection of 40 per cent had been imposed against competing imports from the United Kingdom and 60 per cent against competing imports from all other countries. These policies, which were destined to last for a quarter of a century, made it attractive to establish locally owned industries often carrying out simple manufacturing operations in the production of small batches which were sub optimal by international standards but which could still be made profitable because of the high levels of protection available. The primary focus was on supplying the small Irish market. Manufacturing output grew very slowly and there was mass emigration.

Nineteen-fifty-seven saw the commencement of a fifteen-year

---

* Liam Connellan BE, FIAE, FIEI, LLD (*honoris causa)* was Director General of the Confederation of Irish Industry from 1972 to 1992. He was President of the Royal Dublin Society from 1995 to 1998. He is currently Chairman of Veolia Environmental Companies in Ireland and the Michael Sweetman Educational Trust.

phase which was to prepare industry in Ireland for free trade and entry into the EEC. The first steps were to encourage inward investment and promote exports. The Control of Manufactures Act introduced in 1932 which required that all new manufacturing plants should have majority Irish ownership was repealed. Export profits tax relief—imposing no tax on profits earned from exports—was introduced. Investment in Ireland by foreign owned companies was promoted and as many of them were interested primarily in manufacturing for export markets they were subject to little or no taxation on profits earned. Zero tax on profits was particularly attractive to firms manufacturing products at the most profitable stage in their life cycles.

In 1961 the Irish Government announced its intention to seek membership of the EEC. Then, following the failure of the application by the United Kingdom and Ireland to join the EEC, in 1964 the Government negotiated the Anglo Irish Free Trade Agreement which committed Irish industry to a schedule of reducing tariff barriers of 40 per cent against competing British products over a ten-year period in preparation for eventual membership of a larger free trade area. Irish manufacturers were granted the advantages of Commonwealth Preference on exports to Britain. Established industry had to cope with adapting to significant external pressures each year. As a result of the greater openness of the Irish economy, the encouragement of inward investment, and preferential access to the British market the rate of growth of manufacturing output in Ireland in the period since 1957 doubled from the 3 per cent per annum growth of the previous twenty-five years to about 6 per cent per annum and many new foreign owned manufacturing plants were established. There was a palpable air of confidence in industry, and for the first time since independence, apart from the period of the Second World War, the population started to grow.

This was the environment in which the FII, as the representative organisation for industry, operated in 1964. It was still a small organisation with a total staff of fifteen. It became essential that industry should examine how it was organised to meet the emerging challenges. Michael Sweetman joined the Federation in 1964 from Córas Tráchtála (the Irish Export Board) where he was head of the newly formed trade advisory section having returned to Ireland following posts managing the offices of CTT in Canada and New York. He was appointed Director of Information at the Federation.

Early in 1966 leading members of the Federation attended an extraordinary general meeting to discuss how industry might best be represented in an era of participative economic planning which followed the First Programme for Economic Expansion in the late 1950s. Following this meeting an ad hoc group known as the '1966 Business Conference' was formed partly as a result of a call by the Taoiseach, Mr Seán Lemass, that business should accept a broader role in national affairs and in the planning and implementation of the economic development programmes. The group employed US economic consultants who, following extensive study, recommended the formation of a new nationwide Irish business organisation which would represent business in economic and social affairs. The proposal failed because of 'attitudes, involvement and money, in that order of importance'. Nevertheless, it was recognised that the status quo could not be maintained, and the 1967 Annual Report recognised that the Federation would have to adapt and change irrespective of the re-sponse to the consultants' proposals.

An early indication of industrial attitudes to the prospect of EEC membership was given by Guy Jackson in his capacity as President of the Federation in 1967 when he stated:

> On our own we have no power to prevent Ireland becoming a near de-serted island on the fringe of the Atlantic; as a contributing member of the European Community we would be in the mainstream of the world's richest market.

The Federation set about recruiting highly qualified staff to work on policy development and was to more than double its staff in a five-year period. Michael participated as a member of delegations to meet with the Minister for Industry and Commerce on subjects such as price control. But it was as Director of Foreign Trade that his true vision was given its full scope. In 1968 he was the author of a seminal document: *Challenge: Industry and Free Trade*. The first edition was presented to George Colley TD, Minister for Industry and Commerce. It was widely acclaimed as a valuable contribution to the national debate on the potential consequences of free trade in the light of the Anglo Irish Free Trade Agreement and the growing possibility of membership of the EEC. It was described at the time as an 'important independent step by industry on the vital question of research and the evaluation of fundamental requirements for all areas of industry'.

The Federation of Irish Industries changed its name to the Confederation of Irish Industry (CII) in March 1970 when its Memorandum of Association was rewritten to reflect 'the positive and forward approach of the organisation to its role and function in the future' and the Articles of Association were revised to extend the membership base by giving formal 'recognition to the important part to be played by the industrial sector organisations and the affiliated organisations'. Michael was appointed Director of Business Policy in the new organisation.

In 1971 the successor to *Challenge: Industry and Free Trade* entitled *Signpost: Industry in the 1970s* was launched. Once again it won plaudits—this time from *The Irish Times* which noted that 'it violated the rules which prescribe dullness and prolixity for all important documents'.

Meanwhile negotiations had been taking place regarding Ireland's membership of the EEC, and had reached the stage when the proposal had to be put to the people in a referendum in May 1972. The CII declared itself strongly in favour of membership despite the obvious competitive difficulties which membership would pose for the traditional sectors of industry, many of which were capable of surviving only with the protection of high tariff barriers. A broader view of the overall benefits to the whole economy and the potential for increased foreign direct investment prevailed. This viewpoint was clearly expressed in an authoritative 1968 study conducted by the FII supporting EEC membership, and quoted by Michael during the campaign prior to the 1972 referendum, which concluded with the statement:

> If we are prepared to take courageous decisions now and implement energetically the policies which the situation demands, then industry will emerge in the 1970s more vigorous than ever before.

Given the strongly pro-EEC stance of the CII which was so ably articulated by Michael and his colleagues it was no surprise that he was willing to transfer on secondment as Director of the Irish Council of the European Movement in July 1971 to spearhead a national campaign in favour of membership.

The European Movement was established in the late 1940s at the same time as the Council of Europe. Its purpose was to promote the

concept of European unity and cooperation as an alternative to conflict. There were branches in most Western European countries and
the Irish branch was established in 1955. In 1961 it had supported the
decision to apply for EEC membership. It enjoyed the support of all
the main political parties, and its membership included trade unions,
industrial and commercial bodies, as well as numerous organisations
and private individuals.

Michael set about the task of promoting membership of the EEC
with vigour and enthusiasm. He spoke at a myriad of meetings promoting the vision of an Ireland as a full and confident participating
member of the EEC. He addressed meetings throughout the length
and breadth of the country.

In an article in the *Irish Press* in March 1972 he argued the benefits
for agriculture:

> In Ireland 27 per cent of the work force are still in agriculture. This is the
> strongest economic argument for full membership. As full members the
> value of our present agricultural exports to Britain and the EEC would
> be increased by at least 80 million pounds per year, while at the same
> time present Irish Government subsidies between 30-40 million pounds
> per year to farmers would no longer be necessary. This would have very
> far-reaching effects on the prosperity of the whole community, resulting
> in many thousands of new jobs in Irish industry and services and more
> resources for bringing our social services closer to the standards of Britain
> and the EEC.

In relation to industry he pointed out:

> We could secure free entry to the EEC market for our industrial ex-
> ports under a free trade agreement of the kind now being negotiated by
> Sweden, Switzerland, Austria, and Finland. Such an agreement would
> of course involve removing protection for Irish industry on the home
> market. If on the other hand, as is sometimes advocated, we wanted to
> retain protection on the home market for Irish industry, we would have to
> sacrifice free access for our exports to EEC markets. Some 40,000 jobs in
> Irish industry depend directly on industrial exports. On the other hand,
> according to the Committee on Industrial Organisation not more than
> 10,000 industrial jobs need be lost as a result of removing protection. In
> this choice between retaining protection or free access to export markets
> the balance of advantage seems clearly in favour of the latter.

He dismissed the option of associate membership rather than full
membership in a speech on 15 October 1971 when comparing the deal

being offered to non-candidate countries such as Sweden and Switzerland:

> Now that the EEC has formulated its proposals for these countries it is much easier to examine this alternative in detail than it was a few months ago. The kind of arrangement emerging for Sweden is that she would adopt virtually all full Common Market membership requirements in the industrial sector but would stay out of agricultural policy and political decision taking.

On political developments he expressed the hope that the decade would see the emergence of a European federal system controlled by a democratically elected parliament.

> If that is achieved one effect will be the reassertion of their identity by many of the smaller European peoples who have been more or less held down by the present structure of nation states. Regions will become more important as the absolute dominance of the national state declines.

In an article in the *Tablet* in March 1972 he saw European unity as a means of breaking away from narrow nationalism:

> The ideal of European unity is an effort to break away from the various nationalisms which have done such incalculable harm to the peoples of Europe over the past century. Nationalism when it bursts through as a desire to kill and destroy others (as it has done in Ireland no less than in every other part of Western Europe), is a vicious thing. Fifty million dead in Europe this century are mute witnesses to that. Too often we have confused patriotism, a legitimate love of one's homeland, with nationalism, which so often shows as a hatred of others. It is my belief that in learning to live with the other peoples of Europe, we in Ireland will learn to live in peace with each other.

A pamphlet authored by him as Director of the Irish Council of the European Movement, *The European Community: Why Ireland Should Join,* argued that:

> The EEC was established because a number of leading European statesmen, having seen Europe plunged in the slaughter and devastation of two major wars within thirty years, shared a keen anxiety to build a new order in Europe which would make such disasters less likely, or even impossible in the future. It was clear to these men that it was the division of Europe into independent, selfish and aggressive nation states which was the root cause of these calamitous conflicts. Nationalism as an ideology is, in fact, contrary to belief in the universal brotherhood and equality of men.

He recognised, and accurately forecast that:

Inevitably, removing protection will involve some weeding out of weak and inefficient firms. This means that over the decade, some thousands of people will have to change their jobs. That is not an unhealthy thing. In any vigorous, modern economy some industries are declining and others are growing. That is better than the kind of economic stagnation which we have had to endure for so much of the fifty years since independence.

And concluded with the following expression of concern that:

Should we in this generation, turn our backs on the mainstream of European history and condemn this nation to becoming an isolated backwater, it will be a crime not only against ourselves, but against those who went before—some of whom died to win for Ireland a worthy place in the community of nations. We are being offered a chance to take that place. We must not refuse it. We will not be offered it again.

The effectiveness of his role among the population at large, in partnership with that of his colleague E. J. Gray, Director-General of the Confederation, and diverse groups in Irish society was rewarded by the remarkable 81 per cent vote in favour of membership.

The referendum on entry to the EEC was held on 10 May 1972. Industry was solidly in favour of entry. In the lead-up to the referendum the CII stated that:

Suffice it to say that CII has always believed that there can be little prospects of a small economy such as ours attaining full employment and raising its living standards to levels comparable with those of advanced European countries, without entering into a free trade environment at some stage or another. Needless to say there can be little future for the 35,000 jobs dependent on exporting firms except in a free trade environment. And since the EEC, in addition to guaranteeing access to virtually limitless markets, also provides exceptional benefits for agriculture, and therefore for industries and services dependent on agriculture, the EEC has always seemed to us an opportune and advantageous route towards free trade ...

It is important to stress, of course, that Irish entry will not, of itself, solve any of the country's problems. The EEC provides an opportunity—an unprecedented and probably unrepeatable opportunity—but an opportunity nonetheless within which our problems of unemployment, low living standards and slow growth can be solved.

At the time industry in Ireland was highly protected against competition from imports. Membership of the EEC would mean that this protection would have to be phased out completely within five years. The problems of many protected industries were epitomised by the footwear industry which in an official report stated:

> The potential advantages of mass production are vitiated—by the large number of sizes, shapes and styles necessary to meet public demand. It is not unusual for the average factory to be producing as many as 150 different designs of shoe at the same time, often in small runs.

In addition, industry was concerned about the suitability of the structure of industrial grants and incentives. A National Industrial and Economic Council report in 1968 had stated that:

> The general purpose of grants, loans and other industrial incentives is to induce investment that might not otherwise have taken place. It is not desirable that State aids should serve as temporary props to the inefficient or should encourage investment that is not self sustaining.

Industry had been planning for entry to Europe. The CII had sent a delegation to Brussels in the autumn of 1971 to assess the need for continuous liaison and representation at various levels. It would be necessary to have day-to-day contact with Commission officials, and with the Irish Commissioner, to keep in touch with Commission thinking on industrial policy and to ensure that there would be a practical awareness of Irish views and problems. The Confederation would have to join UNICE—the European Industry and Employers Confederation—which was in continuous contact with the Commission on issues of industrial concern. It would have to appoint a permanent delegate to UNICE, and to participate fully in its plenary sessions and working parties. It would have to nominate members to the Economic and Social Committee which was representative of industry, employers, trade unions, farmers and consumer interests in the member states, and which the Treaties required should be consulted by the Commission on all proposals for economic and social legislation.

The outcome of this planning pointed to the need to establish a permanent office in Brussels called the Irish Business Bureau. It would be jointly funded by the CII (four-sevenths); the Federated Union of Employers (two-sevenths); and the Association of Chambers of Commerce (one-seventh).

On 18 June, little more than a month after the referendum was passed, a high level Irish business delegation set out from Dublin to Brussels via London in order to make arrangements for the establishment of the Irish Business Bureau, and to have meetings with relevant organisations. Disaster was to strike. Minutes after take-off from Heathrow Airport en route to Brussels the aircraft crashed at Staines claiming the lives of 12 leading Irish businessmen among the 118 people who died in the disaster.

These were: Con Smith, President CII; Guy Jackson, Past President CII; Michael Rigby Jones, Member of Executive Committee CII; Ned Gray, Director General CII; Michael Sweetman, Director of Business Policy CII; Fergus Mooney, Trade Officer CII; Hugh Kilfeather, Córas Tráchtála; Melville Miller, Federated Union of Employers; Ivan Webb, Irish Employers Confederation; Michael O'Reilly, Association of Chambers of Commerce of Ireland; Owen Lochrin, Association of Chambers of Commerce of Ireland; Edward Coleman, Cork Chamber of Commerce.

The loss of so many key industrial leaders at such a crucial time was an immense setback. The CII *Newsletter* of 11 July commented:

> We are still too near the events and the men to be able to do justice to their achievements. That must come later. It is indeed difficult to find the heart and will to resume our role; but knowing that we must, we make a new start; a start not from the first beginnings but from a knowledge. . . and representative authority which is the legacy of these men to the Confederation.

And Mr P. J. Keehan , Acting President of the CII stated:

> It is imperative that we should act quickly to recover from this tragedy. This we are determined to do. We owe it to our departed colleagues to follow through what they set out to accomplish. We owe it to our members in these critical months before entry to the European Community.
>
> The greatest single challenge facing Irish industry at present is to prepare for our imminent entry into the EEC. This was the task in which our colleagues were engaged at the time of the accident. We are concerned to add to the impetus of their efforts so as to minimise the effects of the tragedy on the Irish economy. As a tribute to their memory we will ensure by every means in our power that the momentum is maintained.

The CII had now a diminished staff of fewer than 25 people. The task ahead was very great. The Confederation of British Industry (CBI) offered to second its Deputy Director from London. Instead, the author was initially seconded from the Irish Management Institute as Director General ad interim and appointed permanently in

November. Consideration was given to merging the organisation with the Irish Management Institute in order to form a new Confederation of Irish Business but this did not go ahead.

In mid October a new delegation of business representatives visited Brussels for a three-day visit to European institutions. Then on 1 November Mr P. J. Jordan was appointed first Director of the Irish Business Bureau in Brussels with the task of representing Irish business interests to the institutions of the Communities, and of being the 'eyes and ears' of Irish industry in Brussels.

The first five years of EEC membership

Ireland entered the EEC on 1 January 1973. This required the elimination of all tariff protection against competing imports from the other member states within five years, and tariffs against goods from other countries had to be reduced to the Common External Tariff averaging 8 per cent.

On 1 January 1973 the President of the CII in a message to members wrote:

> On this day, when Ireland takes her place with her eight partners in the European Communities, Irish industry takes its position in a market of 250 million people. As part of this large, prosperous and rapidly growing Community, Irish industry has a paramount role in ensuring its fullest economic, social and political development. It is an opportunity industry must not neglect.

The most important consequence for Irish industry was a requirement to phase out all tariff protection against goods from other member states within five years. At the time of entry Ireland's tariff against goods coming from the United Kingdom was 16 per cent, and was 60 per cent against goods coming from other member states. In addition it would be necessary to reduce the tariff against goods from outside the EEC from an average of 60 per cent to the Common External Tariff level of 8 per cent.

An important early emphasis was the necessity for Irish firms to get involved with their European level trade associations. Michael Smurfit, Managing Director of the Jefferson Smurfit Group, gave an early instructive example of the benefits:

> Let me give you one example of how one industry with which I am as-

sociated got on the inside track quickly. Three years ago, the industry formed an Irish institute with the specific task of getting to know their European competitors, and the major producers in each country. We obtained representation on their main committees which were statistical, economic, technical, and marketing. Within two years the Irish companies had sufficient data to determine completely the relative efficiency of their respective European counterparts. This information also helped the industry to determine its European goals within the EEC, and has also been of use in discussion with trade unions and work people in motivation, manning, and productivity deals because exact comparison could be made.

Industry groups in Ireland should, therefore, become involved with their European counterparts. This costs money, but it can be extremely rewarding in understanding, not only one's own future competitors, but also the environment in which they operate.

As had been predicted by Michael Sweetman there was renewed interest in cross-Border cooperation and discussions between industry in the Republic and Northern Ireland were intensified. During the first year of membership two formal meetings were held between representatives of the CII and the Northern Ireland branch of the CBI to explore mutually beneficial issues. These meetings would culminate many years later in the formation of a Joint Business Council between the two organisations.

By the end of 1977 Irish industry was operating in a free trade zone comprising 250 million people. It had been a measure of the growing self confidence of manufacturers in Ireland that they campaigned strongly for membership of the EEC. The wisdom of this approach was borne out by the continued expansion of industry during the five-year transition period to free trade. While the traditional sectors of industry experienced a decline in output this was more than counterbalanced by the growth of an emerging high technology sector (comprising information technology, electronics, chemicals and pharmaceuticals) and overall manufacturing output continued to expand by a healthy 6 per cent annually. The industrial sector had coped successfully with a massive step change.

The predictions of Michael Sweetman and his colleagues were vindicated. Despite a rapid reduction of tariff barriers industry in Ireland sustained a growth rate similar to that which it had experienced throughout the 1960s. Irish exports were diversified. Dependence on exports to the United Kingdom fell from two thirds to one half during the first five years of membership, and the share of Irish exports to other EEC countries doubled. The annual growth in the output of the Irish economy which had lagged that of the EEC over the fifteen years prior to entry grew more rapidly than the European average during this critical transition phase. These trends which were based on a growing manufacturing sector continued until the end of the century.

Irish manufacturing firms had to cope with a wide variety of changes in the decades since independence. The protectionist phase which commenced in the early 1930s played a significant role in establishing a manufacturing base. However, small-scale manufacture for a market of less than 3 million was uncompetitive. The Anglo Irish Free Trade agreement of 1964 which started the process of dismantling tariffs put many firms under pressure. Competition intensified for traditional industries. This had been foreseen by Michael and his colleagues who supported entry to the EEC although it would exacerbate the difficulties faced by many sectors. While many firms making traditional products perished they were replaced by high tech manufacturers from abroad, and the industrial base continued to expand. In the final year of the 1970s participation in the European Monetary System required the Irish Government to manage an independent currency for the first time, and laid the foundation for adoption of the euro over twenty years later.

The attitudes of the population became more outward looking and self assured with higher education levels, successful membership of the European Union, more travel abroad resulting from inexpensive air travel and access to information technology which eliminated lingering perceptions of peripherality. Problems were there to be solved and obstacles to be overcome. Experience had shown that the only constant was change. The key ingredient for success in the future as in the past would be how that change was managed.

The Michael Sweetman Educational Trust

In the aftermath of the Staines air disaster a group of friends and admirers of Michael decided to establish an Educational Trust which came formally into being on 7 June, 1975. Since then the Trust has operated under the auspices of the Irish Council of the European Movement (now called the European Movement)

The Trust Deed states that:

It has been decided to establish a charitable trust to be called 'The Michael Sweetman Educational Trust' with a view to perpetuating the memory of his outlook and achievements, with particular emphasis on the encouragement of the Irish people to achieve an understanding of and to participate in European affairs.

An appeal was launched on 2 October 1974 to enable the public to subscribe to the Michael Sweetman Educational Trust for the purpose of providing awards to enable persons from Ireland to attend colleges, universities or educational institutions in Europe.

An appeal committee would receive subscriptions and donations to implement the terms of the Trust Deed. The Trust Deed was between the First Trustees and the Second Trustees (the Appeal Committee). There were seven First Trustees as follows: Barbara Sweetman FitzGerald, Garret FitzGerald, Patrick Lynch, Donal Nevin, Michael Flanagan, Donal Flynn, and Neville Keery. The Second Trustees or Appeal Committee members were: Thomas Garvey, Michael Flanagan, Donal Flynn, Paul Hogan, Frank O'Connor, Neville Keery.

The first tranche of subscriptions amounted to a total of £10,000 which provided an initial capital base for the Trust. Annual operating expenses would be met from the investment income.

The first year of the essay competition was 1976. The four winning students were awarded with a two-week visit to the Continent, accompanied by Loman Conway, CEO, Sligo VEC. They came from counties Carlow, Cork, Dublin and Sligo. Speaking at a lunch in Leinster House to wish them bon voyage the Attorney General Declan Costello said that he was 'particularly honoured to be associated with this memorial to Michael Sweetman. Indeed the subject of the essay competition set by the Trust concerning the significance of the Lomé Convention, is most appropriate. Michael was always concerned for those who needed assistance and for the underprivileged'. The group visited the European Parliament in Luxembourg, the Irish Representation in Brussels, the Belgian Parliament, the ARBED Steelworks in Luxembourg, the College of Europe in Bruges and the Rungis meat market in Paris.

In almost every year since, until 2000, scholarships were awarded to four students usually based on the results of an essay competition. Then in 2001 the Trust linked up with the Euroscola Programme operated by the European Parliament. This included attendance at the Parliament and participation in a young people's parliament during which key European issues were debated with groups from other EU countries. This arrangement enabled groups of about 25 Irish students accompanied by three teachers to visit Strasbourg for three days.

A further evolution of the operation of the Trust came in 2005 when it focused its applications on Leaving Certificate Applied students attending Vocational Schools and Youth Reach Centres. The Trust continues to select the successful students arising from their Contemporary Issues Task module (project work having a European dimension). The visit is funded partially by the Vocational Education Committee in the home county of each successful applicant through the Irish Vocational Education Association, and also by the Euroscola programme operated by the European Parliament. The experience gained by the participants in acquiring a better understanding of the European Union, together with a growing confidence in their ability to participate in discussions with other members of the group and those from other countries at the Parliament, have both been invaluable. For many of the scholarship winners the visit to the European Parliament provides the first opportunity of visiting mainland Europe and has given them a brief exposure to European affairs, social, cultural, political and economic. Many of the students have had their later performance and career choices profoundly influenced by the experience.

Loman Conway continues to contribute hugely to the organisation and selection process each year. The members of the Trust in 2009 were: Barbara FitzGerald, Dr Garret FitzGerald, Dr Peter Sutherland, Liam Connellan (Chairman), Loman Conway, Donal Nevin, Neville Keery, Michael Peart, and Patrick Sweetman. It is a fitting tribute to the heritage and prescience of Michael Sweetman that his exceptional foresightedness and commitment are commemorated a full generation after the disaster of 18 June 1972 by providing encouragement and assistance to young Irish people to participate actively in the European Union. His vision and influence live on.

Note: Some paragraphs in the early part of this chapter draw heavily on *The Confederation of Irish Industry: The First Fifty Years 1932–1982* by J. W. O'Hagan and G. F. Foley.

A persuasive patriot

T. K. Whitaker*

Michael Sweetman was one of the ablest of the elite group of dedicated promoters of Ireland's progress who lost their lives in an air crash near London in June 1972, en route to Brussels in contemplation of Ireland's entry to the European Community. He was only thirty-six years of age but had already played an impressive part in the promotion of industry, trade and social reform. With Alexis FitzGerald, James Meenan, Declan Costello, and others he was one of the 'think tank' enlightening and guiding Fine Gael policy.

Patriotism, competence and persuasiveness informed his pioneering work with Córas Tráchtála, the Federation of Irish Industries and the Irish Council of the European Movement. No doubt it was due to his influence that, in a contemporary tussle with the Department of Industry and Commerce, I was able to warn that Department against being more protectionist than the FII!

A reminder of the 'dark night of the soul' which prevailed when Michael and I, in our particular contexts, were trying to improve the economic and social scene in Ireland is given by the following 'main anxieties' mentioned in *Economic Development* fifty years ago:

1) Since 1951 emigration has been proceeding at a rate which not merely neutralises the natural increase but actually causes a net drop in population, with depressing psychological and economic effects.

2) The rate of increase in real national income is much lower than in Britain and in Europe generally, a fact which reinforces the tendency to emigrate.

3) Savings are small and irregular and even the low rate of domestic capital formation in the past would not have been achieved but for the use of

---

* T. K. Whitaker is a former economist and public servant, credited with a pivotal role in the economic development of Ireland. In 1956 at the age of 39 he was appointed Secretary of the Department of Finance.

external reserves which are now greatly depleted.

4) Domestic investment is not directed sufficiently towards immediately productive purposes.

5) In association with the foregoing are to be found relatively high taxation and low productivity, insufficient training in management and supervision, excessive restrictionism and inadequate technical knowledge.

This was the scene in which Michael played a reformist role until his premature death.

Half a century later, we can record major improvements in life expectancy and living standards and look forward, as the present recession is overcome, to regaining what Churchill liked to call 'the broad sunlit uplands'.

Young Fine Gaelers

John Bruton*

Michael Sweetman was an influence in my political life from the time I left school and first began to become directly involved in politics. I joined Fine Gael in Dunboyne in September 1965 and shortly afterwards I also joined the students' branch in UCD.

I also became involved in an organisation called the Fine Gael Youth Group, which had been formed in 1964 to mobilise young canvassers for the Galway by-election in which John Donnellan was triumphantly elected to the Dáil as a Fine Gael candidate. Michael Sweetman was actively involved in the Fine Gael Youth Group and I first met him at one of their meetings in the Prince of Wales Hotel in Athlone.

I became National Secretary of the Youth Group in 1966 and we tried to transform it into a national organisation with regional and constituency structures, rather than simply a ginger group of young canvassers ready to travel to by-elections. We did not really succeed in this but the group provided an entry point for many young people into Fine Gael politics and caused quite a stir at the Fine Gael Árd Fheis in 1968. Members of the Youth Group had motions placed on the order paper that were controversial, and persuaded two TDs, Paddy Harte and Surgeon Hogan, to force a contest for some of the elective positions at the Árd Fheis to which 'headquarters' nominees would previously have been elected unopposed. This sort of thing would not happen at party conferences today and is testament to the openness of the then leadership of Liam Cosgrave.

I also met Michael during the 1966 Presidential election campaign of Tom O'Higgins. It is hard to exaggerate the morale-boosting effect of the success of this campaign on Fine Gael. After a disappoint-

---

* John Bruton was elected to the Dáil in 1969 at the age of 22. He became Fine Gael party leader in 1990 and Taoiseach, 1994-1997. He is a Former EU ambassador to Washington and has been Chairman of the IFSC since May 2010.

ing general election in 1965, Tom O'Higgins was able, by mounting a modern and future-oriented campaign, to get within only 10,000 votes of unseating Éamon de Valera. I believe Michael played a big part in developing the intellectual and rhetorical content of Tom O'Higgins' great campaign.

Michael was very knowledgeable about economic questions as he held a senior position in the Confederation of Irish Industry (CII). He made that knowledge generously available to his friends in Fine Gael. Not only was he helpful to younger members of the party, but he also won the trust of the party leader, Liam Cosgrave, to the extent that he contributed to many of Mr Cosgrave's important speeches.

At the time, the business world seemed to be dominated by our political opponents, and people involved in Fine Gael felt themselves to be almost a marginalised minority. In some places, party meetings were held in private houses for fear of drawing undue attention to the political affiliation of those attending. Tom O'Higgins' campaign began to dispel that mentality. But it also meant a lot to have someone like Michael Sweetman, who was visibly at the centre of economic decision-making in the country, involved with the party.

One reason that Irish business had been dominated by our political opponents was that many of the leading businesses had grown up under the regime of protective tariffs and import licences, put in place by Seán Lemass after 1932, and this regime had had the effect of making business quite dependent on the party in power to get a sufficiently high tariff to keep out competition or to get import licences which conferred a quasi-monopoly on the licence holder. Protectionism cultivated a dependency culture.

By 1965, all that was beginning to change. Seán Lemass himself, as Taoiseach, led the reversal of his own old protectionist policies. Major studies were being undertaken on how different Irish industries might adapt to free trade conditions and, through his role in CII, Michael Sweetman was playing a central role in that work.

The Anglo Irish Free Trade Agreement was negotiated in 1966, and the possibility of Ireland joining the European Common Market was canvassed by Seán Lemass, with the active support of Fine Gael leaders James Dillon and Liam Cosgrave. I believe Michael Sweetman provided support and arguments to bring Fine Gael in the pro-European direction it was taking. Prior to that, Fine Gael would have had a more transatlantic orientation in its external policy. He believed that by moving towards a closer connection with continental Europe Ireland could develop a more mature, balanced and less dependent relationship with Britain, which would help in resolving past differences. Subsequently, in his last campaign before his tragic death, Michael played a leading role in persuading the Irish people to endorse joining the Common Market in the referendum of 1972.

I have a vivid memory of one occasion in 1967 when I called on Michael's help to make the argument for a closer engagement with Europe.

I was actively involved in the party in Meath and was constantly on the lookout for ways of getting the party's message (and my own name!) into the local paper, the *Meath Chronicle*. I saw that the anti-Common Market Campaign was organising a public meeting in the Central Hotel in Navan to make its case that Ireland should stay out of the Common Market, even if Britain joined. The meeting was to be addressed by Anthony Coughlan and to be chaired by Seán Mac Stiofáin, the Sinn Féin President of the time, who lived near Navan.

An old school friend of mine and I decided that we would go along to the public meeting and make a case that contradicted the view of the meeting's organisers. In retrospect this seems to be an impudent thing to have done, but we at least felt comfortable going to the Central Hotel because all our own Fine Gael meetings were held there too and the owner, Mattie Crinion was a party sympathiser.

Before going to the meeting I decided I should consult Michael Sweetman on the best arguments I could make in favour of Ireland joining the Common Market. I asked him if he could give me a list of Ireland's principal industrial exports to Britain, which were by then admitted tariff-free under the Anglo Irish Free Trade Agreement, and to give me the Common Market tariff on each of these same products, so that I could argue that, if Britain joined the Common Market and Ireland stayed out, our exports of these products to Britain and Northern Ireland would be penalised by having to pay extra tariffs. Michael produced a very impressive list from which I was able to highlight Meath products, like furniture and carpets.

After Anthony Coughlan had finished his address, I stood up in the body of the audience and asked to be allowed to make a case. Seán Mac Stiofáin gave me the floor. I started, at some length, to go through my arguments and the figures Michael had given me. This was too much for an elderly Sinn Féin supporter in the audience who did not like to see an opponent taking over their meeting. He started tapping his walking stick on the floor. Referring to my family's background in the cattle raising business, he shouted an old slogan from the Economic War—'The bullock for the road, and the land for the people'. In other words, he was telling me I should shut up. At this point, Seán Mac Stiofáin intervened and insisted that there would be free speech at the meeting and that I would get a full hearing, which I did. This showed another side to Seán MacStiofáin to the one most often portrayed in accounts of his controversial career.

Subsequently, I supplied a script of my remarks to the *Meath Chronicle* and the paper devoted almost a whole page to the debate, with Anthony Coughlan's speech down one side and my own down the other. This was a breakthrough of a kind for a twenty-year-old like myself, who had never at that stage been elected to anything, and it helped give me the confidence and the profile to launch myself into electoral politics in Meath two years later.

And when I was elected to the Dáil in June 1969, the official declaration of my election was made by Michael's father, Paddy Sweetman, who as County Registrar was Returning Officer for the general election in the Meath constituency. Michael himself was a candidate in the same general election, one of four Fine Gael candidates put forward to contest the seat in Dublin North West vacated by Declan Costello.

Fine Gael was a divided party during Michael's ten-year career, with noisy arguments going on between proponents and opponents of the Just Society document produced to the Fine Gael front bench by Declan Costello in 1964. The original document was long and technical, with detailed sections on social capital investment and central banking. Many of those who argued most heatedly about it, had probably never read it. In fact it is very difficult to find a copy. The Just Society became more a symbol than a policy to be studied and implemented.

Michael's genius in these years was that he was able to bridge these divisions. He had read and contributed to the Just Society policy document, but he was also able to win the trust and confidence of more conservative members of the party, and of Liam Cosgrave and Gerard Sweetman, his formidable cousin—whose 1956 budget started the process of building Ireland as an export-oriented economy by exempting export profits from corporation tax.

Michael Sweetman achieved much in a very short life. He achieved it through his influence on others, a quiet persuasive authority without show or bluster. He was not without ambition, I am sure, but he knew that often one can achieve more in politics by letting other people take credit than by insisting on taking it oneself.

Reminiscence of shared interests

Bruce Arnold*

I first met Michael Sweetman in 1968. I was then working as a free-lance journalist. I wrote a political column for Nicholas Leonard, who was editor of *Business and Finance*, and consulted Michael on some stories. Since 1966 I had been doing intermittent broadcasting for RTÉ, both radio and television. Among other commissions I interviewed Dr Richard Hayes at the time of Alfred Chester Beatty's death in January 1968. Hayes, the former Director of the National Library, had become Keeper of the Chester Beatty Library and knew Beatty well. After the 1969 general election I worked as a speech writer for Charles Haughey and in the Department of Finance on the popular version of the Third Programme for Economic Expansion, published in March 1969.

Michael was Director of Foreign Trade for the Federation of Irish Industries under Jim Stacey. He asked me if I would do part-time press and publicity work for the organisation and I agreed to this, reporting through him to Jim Stacey and discussing the work of the organisation with the various sector heads.

Change was in the air. Entry into the Common Market was the great challenge and the energising of industry, commerce and the economy generally was exercising the minds of those on the council of the Federation, led at the time by a group that included Guy Jackson, of Guinness, Michael Rigby Jones, of Irish Ropes, Christopher Aliaga-Kelly and others. At the time, the Federated Union of Employers was a separate organisation, its Director General Dan McAuley, and this division was seen as a weakness in the growing climate of industrial confrontation exemplified by lengthy bank strikes in 1966 and 1970.

The man who negotiated, with considerable skill, on behalf of the

* Bruce Arnold is a writer and journalist, writing about politics.

banks during that dispute was Ned Gray, and it was no surprise, when the Federation of Irish Industries was reorganised as the Confederation of Irish Industry, that he became its Director General. This was in 1969–70. The planning and motivation of this major step in strengthening the voice of industrialists, employers and those who were to aid in the process of taking Ireland into Europe involved me with Ned Gray on the various issues of press relations and publicity. I discussed with Michael and then proposed to Ned that we needed a weekly newsletter that would be circulated to all members but would also go to the media, politicians, ministers and heads of the semi-state bodies that largely ran the country. This was an effective strategy. It made it possible for the organisation to set an agenda rather than responding to events with hastily drafted press statements.

Fairly regularly, Ned, Michael and I would meet to discuss the major editorial points to be made to members. Even when a wider audience was aimed at the collegiality of the membership was never overlooked. This led to a demand from members for more contact and Michael and I organised meetings with members in different parts of the country.

We would frequently spend time together, usually exploring wider issues, one of which concerned his main passion at the time—the preparing of Ireland, at every level, for the challenges of Europe. This work of preparation was central to the Confederation's work. I use the word passion with care. Michael was an urbane man with a cool and restrained way of addressing the world. He had a rich sense of humour and privately he expressed his reservations about people and political groupings often with a mixture of disdain and relish. At one level he thought the idea of Ireland in Europe was monumentally absurd. The willingness to change was simply not there. It was a fearsome prospect and involved a huge shifting of minds and hearts. But a far stronger determination to alter the country's mind and bring about the changes that were required prevailed eventually. The two views, with which I broadly concurred, produced many funny experiences and judgements and made working with him an exciting and stimulating activity.

The professional relationship soon developed into a personal friendship. We were roughly the same age. We both had growing families. Our wives got on well. Barbara and Mavis were good cooks,

Michael was a wine enthusiast and knowledgeable on the subject and I was enthusiastic to learn. He and I were keenly interested in politics. We were also interested in social and international affairs.

It was an odd conjunction. Michael and Barbara were devout Catholics. We were equally devout Protestants. He was scion of a distinguished Irish family. I was very English. Difference enhanced friendship.

Another force that gave further thrust to our work was the personality of Ned Gray, the Director General of the Confederation of Irish Industry. He was more than ten years older than us and widely experienced in public service, having worked in the Revenue and the Department of Industry and Commerce before moving to the Industrial Development Authority. He had then worked for the banks during a particularly gruelling time which included one protracted strike.

Despite his seniority and experience he was a great listener and always gave the impression that he would learn by this approach. But he was not specially attuned to the ways in which the press could be guided onto his side in the new role he occupied. Representation was a relatively modern concept and the ways in which the media interpreted the work of organisations such as the Confederation had to be watched closely. Ned increasingly tested his views with Michael and myself. I drafted speeches for him and wrote press releases. These were examined by Michael and then brought to discussion sessions in Ned's office in Ely Place. The same approach applied to the not infrequent applications for help or for legal changes which went to government departments or to individual politicians.

Unlike the two men with whom I worked closely at this time, I remained part-time. I was still, first and foremost and in my own mind, a journalist and the main skills I brought were always within that construction. This was not universally the case by any means. Friends from my time in *The Irish Times*, like Cathal O'Shannon, Alan Montgomery and Tony Kelly, had all moved from full-time involvement in newspaper work to appointments as press officers in corporations. I had no intention of going that way. This was not particularly because of journalism but because, behind all that, I was endeavouring to write fiction and preparing for the publication of my first book, *A Concise History of Irish Art*.

The period of our friendship, which lasted for about three years, was an intensely happy time. Of course many different forces acted on my development, as journalist, as writer, in coming to terms belatedly with a life in Ireland that seemed set to be—and was indeed to become—permanent. This carried with it the reality of relinquishing a future in England, which would have been normal for many of my Trinity College contemporaries. Michael's role in this last transition was to give subtlety and depth to what I had decided.

We discussed Europe and Ireland's future place in it. He was Director of the Irish Council of the European Movement from July 1971 and passionate about the importance of Europe in the country's future. He saw huge problems for Irish agriculture, its industrialisation, its need to modernise, the conflict between profitability and the obsessive concern with land ownership.

He was a member of Fine Gael and a supporter of Declan Costello, to whom he gave help in the drafting of the policy pamphlet, *Towards a Just Society*. In 1969, not long after we had become friends, Michael contested the Dublin North West constituency, failing to gain the seat by the very narrow margin of 160 votes. He longed for a political career and he made his work for the Confederation of Irish Industry 'political' in the best sense of the word, involving a commitment to change and reform, to a more equal, more open society and to a greater share in international affairs.

He also made it political in a more intense, private response to the increasingly alarming events of those years. Though his support was for Declan Costello, within the Fine Gael Party, the party's leader was Liam Cosgrave, a strict 'Law and Order' man and an unbending, old-fashioned Catholic. This led to tensions at a time when the sectarian structure of politics in Northern Ireland was leading towards unprecedented violence such as when the People's Democracy civil rights march at the beginning of January 1969 culminated in the confrontation at Burntollet. The political divergence in the Dáil, barely held under control by Jack Lynch, who had yet to face his first general election as leader of Fianna Fáil, emphasised the shortcomings and the limited understanding at the time of rebellious and liberalising forces that were being unleashed. Michael's analysis of this was immensely valuable to me, as I struggled to understand and write about an unfolding drama that inevitably soon became tragic, with deaths on the streets of Northern Ireland and the threat to the stability of political life in the Republic represented by the 1970 Arms Crisis.

To Michael I give credit for an influence on my judgement and political writing at the time that brought it to the notice of the *Irish Independent*. I was already a prolific freelance contributor to the *Sunday Independent*, edited at that time by Hector Legge. The significant change came from Bartle Pitcher, Managing Director of the group, who was a reader of my *Business and Finance* column on politics, and he invited me to join the staff of the paper as political commentator at the beginning of 1972. We were facing into EEC membership, the Northern Troubles, a general election, and the opportunity led to a smaller role inside the Confederation of Irish Industry. The friendship became more personal, less professional.

Michael was cosmopolitan and sophisticated, but again in the best sense. Our careers, up to that point, had been fundamentally different. His work for Córas Tráchtála, the Irish Export Board, had taken him to Montreal for a time and then to New York, where he headed the CTT offices. And when he returned to Ireland, in 1963, it was to head a newly established trade advisory section. His disposition led naturally on to his place in the Confederation of Irish Industry.

We met often in each other's houses and the discussions ranged more and more widely. The most pleasurable of these concerned wine. Mine was no frivolous induction. Michael was way ahead of his contemporaries in his understanding of the vast subject. His own interest had come about because of two uncles who had started a small wine business some time in the 1940s, creating a cellar at Johnsbrook in Co. Meath. They had displayed great judgement in assembling fine wines, perhaps less judgement in their understanding of the market for what they traded in. This meant that when Michael issued his second wine list in the autumn of 1970 he listed both clarets and burgundies from 'most of the good vintages from 1937 to 1962'. He had also introduced a range of ports which included Cockburn 1904, Dow 1934, Quarles Harris 1937, and three or four shippers of two of the great post-war vintages, of 1955 and 1960, Dow, Taylor, Cockburn, Sandeman, Croft and Graham.

He was a generous host when entertaining and I both drank and bought from him Richebourg 1949, Chambertin 1952, Le Corton 1953 and many clarets from the best years of the 1950s as well as the great 1961s. I still have a bottle of Château Yquem which I bought from him.

Then it all ended, abruptly and tragically, with Michael's death. He was killed in the Trident air crash at Staines on the night of Sunday, 18 June 1972. The plane crashed only minutes after take off from Heathrow. In all 118 people died. At that point it was the worst crash in these islands. The twelve Irish businessmen who perished included Ned Gray, another painful loss. I had worked with all of those who were killed, attending occasional meetings to give press advice, or meeting them individually when they were present for the drafting of statements or policy announcements.

The personal grief over Michael's death lasted many years. I can still summon up, from memory, the rich tone of his voice, the fulsome laughter that was so often part of our private conversation about those we knew through work or politics. He was tall and quite slim. His dark hair was carefully brushed and groomed and he held his head on one side from the habitual bending of his ear for private words with men of lesser stature. There were many of these. His readiness to laugh was an appealing trait, but he could be sharp as well, quick to correct looseness of meaning or error of fact. Conversation with him was always rewarding. The prospect before him, at the time of his death, when he was thirty-six years old, promised a brilliant political career, since that was inevitably where he was directing his energies. He was a great loss to me, a great loss to his family and an immeasurable loss to Ireland.

In memoriam

Moira Woods*

I cannot remember when I first met Michael—it seems now as if I always knew him and Barbara.

It might have been at an anti-Vietnam War demonstration; certainly he was at the anti-war committee meetings: a mixture of pacifists, members of the Labour Party, trade-unionists, Sinn Féin (before the split), Quakers, committed Christians of different denominations, communists, students, teachers. A friend of mine in the Gardaí, many years later, asked me why we were on the Special Branch list in the 1960s. I suppose it might have been those committee meetings.

In the sixties we thought that we could change the world; that governments would listen to the people who had elected them; and Michael epitomised that change.

From a Fine Gael family, Michael was young, handsome, intelligent, someone who was not afraid to challenge the accepted views of his background and class; and his uncle, Michael Sweetman SJ, used to address the crowds in the streets of Dublin at Housing Action meetings. I remember him telling us that his and Barbara's attendance at the anti-war demonstrations did not please some of those from his Fine Gael background—on one occasion James Dillon apologised for the rabble outside the American embassy.

I remember many occasions of laughter, debate, of stimulating discussion. Michael was always open to new ideas, to change. He would discuss, without rancour, different political, theological, philosophical, viewpoints. I am not sure whether he was at Austin Flannery's theological meetings, but he knew other priests and theologians—the Dominicans from the English Slant movement, including the editor of their magazine, Lawrence Bright, Marxist Christians—who were not

* Moira Woods was educated in Burma, Australia, India, England, Africa and Ireland. She is a humanist and pacifist, and was responsible for Donal Foley's initiation of *The Irish Times* series of articles on the Children's Courts.

intimidated by the accepted orthodoxy of the Irish Roman Catholic Church. He was not afraid to think for himself, perhaps the most important gift that he handed on to his children; and this was the most refreshing aspect of one's contact with Michael. The 1950s and 1960s of the last century were a time when few were brave enough in Ireland to speak honestly or openly.

I remember having discussions about the European Community. I was secretary of the Irish Pacifist Movement at the time; we were the Irish section of War Resisters International, and used to receive *Peace News* (the paper of the English section), as well as other pacifist literature, and the message was very firm, 'Butter not Guns'; this was because we thought that Ireland would be forced to participate in a European army. So we were going to vote No when there was a referendum.

Somehow Michael must have sensed our position, because one evening there was a knock at the door, and he appeared, in country disarray and muddy wellington boots, and passionately started to defend the position of Ireland's entry into Europe. I showed him the pacifist literature that we had, and he asked could he take it. (When it came to the referendum, I had changed my mind, mainly influenced by an article in *The Irish Times* by Mary Holland). But it was typical of Michael that he would go to the trouble of arriving and immediately carry on a conversation that had never actually begun: that I think is the definition of real friendship, that one does not have to be in constant communication, but one can continue discussions which may or may not have been started.

We were sure that he would be the next Fine Gael Taoiseach, and Ireland might have been a very different country now if he had not died.

I still treasure two of the books that he gave me: *The Epic of Gilgamesh*, and *The Wall has Two Sides*.

Ave atque Vale.

Gone fishing

Patrick Sweetman

We had set out early, my father and I, my father with the dinghy, not yet inflated, under his arm.

I trudged along with all the other paraphernalia required for the day: fishing rod, tackle bag, pump, Tiffin, two two-piece plastic oars, long coils of rope. Our oilskins squeaked as we brushed through the heather, his olive green, mine canary yellow.

This was to be a new departure. My father had fished many of the Donegal lakes with his father, brother David, and Uncle Hugh. It seemed the more inaccessible the lake, the greater the attraction. This one was miles over bog, visited by sheep, rarely by humans.

An overcast day, stiff wind blowing, perfect conditions for what he had planned.

The dingy inflated, a good size stone was carefully selected to which the rope was securely tied. I was the anchorman. We launched, the boat bobbing alarmingly under Daddy's weight as he plunged aboard. The wavelets on the lake battered the edges of the rubber dingy, the stumpy oars ineffective against the wind. We manoeuvred to the centre of the lake, the sky darkening now. The stone went over the side and to the bottom. For hours I sat, perched precariously on one end of the inflatable yellow dingy, playing the rope out, hand over hand.

The rod (only one for this mission—the anchorman had no free hand) already assembled, was taken up, the line freed to the wind and the carefully selected flies dropped gently on the water. I let out the rope, hand over hand, heeding the instructions as to speed and length, as we drifted down the lake.

When the rope was out, I reversed the process, drawing the rope back in, cold and wet, tugging the boat against the wind. Daddy sat, silently, concentrating on the line, intensely eyeing the water, waiting for the bite. Once he shifted position and the boat lurched. He lost balance and almost rolled over the inflated ring of the boat's side. A good soaking, but no harm done. He laughed.

For hours I hauled the rope in, I let it out, my eleven-year-old hands numb with the cold of the water. I knew little of his other worlds, of Ireland and its history, of its journey to statehood, its journey to maturity, and of the part my father played. I had no need to know.

We caught no fish that day. That perfect day.

Michael Sweetman and the
Just Society [1]

Ciara Meehan*

The Just Society concept embodies in contemporary terms the highest ideals
of those who fought to establish the state. This election is an exciting opportunity to make a reality of the Just Society's two basic principles—freedom
and equality. Freedom today means giving to every citizen the fullest opportunity to participate in government in the shaping of his own life. Equality
means a just sharing of the community's increasing prosperity between all
citizens. This contrasts with the situation under the present government
where the gap is rapidly widening between those who have plenty and those
who have little. This is the situation which Fine Gael is determined to change.
(From a speech by Michael Sweetman in 1969)

This speech, delivered by Michael Sweetman to a meeting of election workers in Phibsboro during the 1969 general election, represented more than the official party line; it was a genuine expression
of his own views on society. As Tom O'Higgins—Minister for Health
in the fifteenth Dáil, (1954–7) TD for Laois-Offaly and later Dublin South, and supporter of the Just Society—recalled, 'he was liberal
in outlook, with a burning zeal for social justice and an intellectual
capacity to indicate achievable reforms'. He was part of a growing
liberal wing of Fine Gael that challenged the party's traditional conservatism. However, as is the case with backroom politics, his role and
influence was not always publicly visible and are not easily traceable.
Nonetheless, as a speech writer, policy adviser, candidate for the Dáil
and subsequently the Seanad, Michael Sweetman played an important role in promoting the concept of social justice.

1 I am grateful to Dr Paul Rouse for his comments on this chapter.

* Ciara Meehan is an IRCHSS Postdoctoral Fellow at the UCD School of History
and Archives. She is currently working on a study of the impact of the Just Society
policy document on Irish politics and society between 1964 and 1987. She is also the
author of *The Cosgrave Party: A History of Cumann na nGaedheal* (Dublin 2010).

The 1960s witnessed a period of social and political change throughout the western world. Social change was experienced in Ireland with the arrival of television and the impact of Vatican II, and Fianna Fáil's Seán Lemass had brought about economic change, but no comparative innovative thinking was on the political agenda. The 'young tigers'—the label given to younger, progressive members—of Fine Gael viewed Irish contemporary politics as incompatible with this more confident society. Declan Costello articulated a new political idea, representative of an educated, younger and more liberal elite. Costello's profile as the son of a former Taoiseach from a privileged background makes him an unlikely figure to have championed the cause of social justice. However, having been elected to Dáil Éireann in 1951 for Dublin North West, he witnessed the effects of poverty, unemployment and emigration, which were widespread in that constituency. Costello also read widely on the subject of social affairs, and was particularly influenced by French post-war reconstruction. His ideas were embodied in the Just Society policy document, the aim of which was to make a reality the concepts of freedom and equality. Among the proposals were plans for a Department of Economic Affairs and a social development strategy that would complement economic modernisation. The document, which had international parallels, essentially represented recognition of a more liberal Ireland.

By the time that Costello took his ideas to the Fine Gael front bench in 1964, the party had been in government for only six of the previous thirty-two years. It was dominated by an older, conservative leadership that was either unwilling or unable to change, and Costello was aware that his views were not shared by the majority of the front bench. The frustration which Declan Costello felt at this time was very much shared by Michael Sweetman. Costello appealed to his colleagues on two grounds: firstly, that his policies were the right ones for Ireland, and secondly, that they offered Fine Gael an opportunity to define its role in Irish politics. The debate took place over a number of weeks, in which nearly every deputy participated, and reached its climax after the document was leaked to the newspapers, with the result that a conclusion had to be arrived at. A policy committee, chaired by Liam Cosgrave—TD for Dún Laoghaire-Rathdown and future leader—was to be established to examine the proposals further. It met in the latter part of 1964 and early 1965, and when the 1965 general election was announced, the documents that the committee had been working on were put before the parliamentary party. The full document—which amounted to several thousand words—was then condensed and adopted as the party's manifesto, entitled *Towards a Just Society*.

The Just Society document was new for Fine Gael. Progressive, forward-looking and with minimal references to Fianna Fáil, it signalled a break with the past. And although some speakers still referred to the party's role as the founders of the state, the preoccupation with the past that had previously characterised Fine Gael rhetoric was largely overcome. In 1965 Fine Gael sought office to 'work towards a society in which freedom and equality are not concepts from an academic textbook, but are expressed in real and tangible conditions which all . . . people can enjoy'. *Towards a Just Society* referred to the 'very wide areas in . . . society where great poverty exists, poverty which is degrading and capable of remedy; [to] appalling housing conditions; [to] totally inadequate health and educational facilities'. The document proposed reforms in the field of economics, changes to the Dáil and Seanad, an increase in the number of schools and teachers, an extension of health services and a choice of doctor for all, changes to social welfare, and protection from unfair prices and unfair trading. In the words of James Dillon—TD for Monaghan and party leader between 1959 and 1965—Fine Gael wanted to bring the country 'safely through into a new era of expansion in a just society with fair shares for all'.

As a member of the policy committee and research staff during the 1965 election, Michael Sweetman did much to assist behind the scenes in the development of the Just Society ideas. But in supporting Costello's proposals, he found himself on the opposing side to his cousin, Gerard Sweetman, the Fine Gael spokesman on finance and also the national director of organisation. The contrast in the outlook of these two men was thrown into starkest relief on this issue; as Garret FitzGerald—who did much to advance the liberal agenda as party leader in the 1980s—observed in his autobiography, the former was a liberal intellectual and the latter a conservative solicitor and businessman. Gerard Sweetman proved to be one of the fiercest opponents of the proposal.

Michael Sweetman's interest in Costello's ideas must have been coloured by his own experience of 1950s Ireland, from which he emigrated to Canada in 1957 after getting married. The Sweetmans were among the 400,000 people who emigrated between 1951 and 1961; a figure that as Enda Delany has noted in his essay 'The Vanishing Irish? The Exodus from Ireland in the 1950s',[2] accounts for almost one-sixth of the total population recorded in 1951. Often described as 'the lost decade', the 1950s were characterised by high levels of emigration, unemployment and general poverty. Michael Sweetman was a very idealistic man who had a sense of the unfairness in society and a desire to make things better. He was particularly concerned with helping those on the bottom of the ladder. It is hardly surprising then that he was attracted to the Just Society ideals.

For the duration of the 1965 general election, Powers Hotel on Kildare Street was home to the Fine Gael campaign press and information centre. The function of that centre was to maintain election propaganda and organise publicity releases to create a certain image of the party. Central to the service was the press bureau, of which Michael Sweetman was a member. In the aftermath of the vote Colonel P. F. Dineen, General Secretary of Fine Gael, wrote to most of those who had worked at the centre during the three week campaign to convey the party's gratitude for their services. Michael Sweetman was praised for his contributions to the creation of advertisements and formulation of suitable slogans.

Although Fine Gael had accepted Costello's policies, endorsement of the manifesto was not wholehearted and James Dillon even appeared to contradict its content at the press launch. The media largely focused its attention on the internal tensions between the party's younger generation and its older, more conservative leadership, with the result that analysis of the policies on offer was often relegated to second place. An *Irish Times* editorial on 19 March, for example, asserted that 'more than once it was rumoured that there was an absolute standstill [with developing the document], with the possibility of resignations and splits', while John Healy—writing as 'Backbencher'—repeatedly criticised the party for being ill-equipped and amateur in its organisation. Furthermore, the Just Society policy arrived too late to be of any real benefit to the party. As Declan Costello once reflected, 'parties don't win elections by policy it puts out three weeks

2 In Dermot Keogh, Carmel Quinlan and Finbarr O'Shea (eds) *The Lost Decade: Ireland in the 1950s* (Cork 2004)

before the election; parties win elections over months and months of work'. Fine Gael's share of the vote rose by only two percentage points, which was not enough to deliver any new seats, and the party remained on the opposition benches.

Although the media had widely criticised Fine Gael for its lack of professionalism and had repeatedly highlighted the internal disunion, Declan Costello's policies began to attract new members to Fine Gael. The air of change was substantiated by the 1966 presidential election, as a consequence of which a more positive atmosphere emerged in the party. During that campaign, Michael Sweetman served as policy adviser and speech writer to the party's candidate Tom O'Higgins. The combination was seen as a formidable one. Michael Sweetman's commitment to Just Society ideals and the promotion of a pluralist society could be clearly identified in many of the speeches given by the Fine Gael candidate. One such speech delivered by O'Higgins at Clones during his whistle-stop tour posed the question, 'Is Ireland a just society?', in answer to which he suggested 'there is much evidence that it is not'. Although Fine Gael was not victorious, O'Higgins came within 10,000 votes—a slim margin for such contests—of defeating the incumbent Éamon de Valera. Colonel Dineen observed how 'we narrowed the gap so drastically as to astonish many of our own supporters and confound the opposition'. Speaking after the result, Liam Cosgrave, now party leader, asserted that the support for O'Higgins was 'a recognition of the positive value of this party's progressive concept of a Just Society which had not sufficient time to make an impact upon the electorate in the 1965 general election'. The liberal wing of the party was strengthened because, as Garret FitzGerald suggested in his autobiography, both the campaign, with its emphasis on a pluralist society, and the close result showed that adventurous policies could win votes.

Declan Costello publicly announced his retirement from politics on 9 February 1967 and although he did not contest the 1969 general election, Fine Gael returned to his Just Society proposals. However, at the time of Costello's retirement *The Citizen*—a party newspaper with the stated aim of supporting Fine Gael only as long as the party was committed to the Just Society—was critical of the lack of development. One article in February 1967 argued that branch meetings were taken up with trivial issues, such as the selling of raffle tickets, while at a national level deputies were more concerned with 'down-ing the "gamblers' government" or with baiting "Charlie" [Haughey], than with describing the Ireland Fine Gael hopes to build on the basis of the Just Society'. The paper advocated a more complete examina-tion and debate of the policy within the parliamentary party and at grassroots level. This never occurred. An attempt to change the party's name to 'Fine Gael: Social Democratic Party' was resisted by Gerard Sweetman on procedural grounds at the 1968 Árd Fheis. Although the majority of delegates appeared to favour the amendment, he argued that it would have to be put to a vote of all members. The postal ballot resulted in an overwhelming rejection of the attempt to formalise the new direction in which the liberal elements were trying to move the party. The event was an interesting microcosm of the struggle between the party's two wings.

Liam Cosgrave had succeeded James Dillon as party leader after the latter resigned in 1965. He was not considered to be as conserva-tive as his predecessor and, as Henry Patterson has noted in *Ireland since 1939*, he was trusted by the traditionalists but was also capable of moving the more liberal proposals forward. Cosgrave's appoint-ments to the front bench in 1965—which included Tom O'Higgins as spokesman on finance and Declan Costello on health and social welfare, as well as the inclusion of Senators Garret FitzGerald and Jim Dooge—prompted *The Irish Times* to comment that 'the new men represent almost a complete takeover by the new generation . . . Mr Cosgrave has done a Lemass on Fine Gael and even gone one bet-ter'. The liberal wing, as part of Cosgrave's strategy to balance both groups, had a clear presence on the front bench. However, he would later become uneasy with the advancement of that group, particularly amidst rumours that there were intentions to replace him as leader. In an unscripted remark during his address to the Árd Fheis of May 1972, he likened the group—which included Garret FitzGerald, Tom O'Higgins, Jim Dooge and Michael Sweetman—to 'mongrel foxes'.

While in Cavan during the 1969 campaign Cosgrave spoke of his pride in counting among the party's ranks 'a splendid array of young men of brilliant intellect—young men who have chosen to take up the Fine Gael standard because they are convinced that in this party their courage and youthful idealism will not be wasted'. Among them was thirty-three year old Michael Sweetman who was attempting to make the transition from the backroom to Dáil deputy. Rather fittingly, the Fine Gael Standing Committee added him to the ticket in the Dublin North West constituency which had been represented by Declan Costello since 1951. Costello was very supportive of the candidacy. According to Paddy Harte's memoirs,[3] Dr Hugh Byrne was approached to stand based on the presumption—correctly as it turned out—that he would take a seat for the party. However, Mary Maher opined in *The Irish Times* that Michael Sweetman was perhaps the obvious successor to Costello's mantle. Although she was suggesting that he might be Costello's successor in the seat, she was clearly implying that he was an heir to Costello's liberal policies. Maher also suggested that Michael Sweetman's presence could siphon off a sizeable amount of liberal, non-party votes that might otherwise have gone to David Thornley of the Labour Party.

The 1969 manifesto—*Winning Through to a Just Society*—reaffirmed the ideas laid out in its 1965 predecessor, but on this occasion the leadership appeared more supportive of the policies. Although Gerard Sweetman tended to make only indirect references and generally refrained from using the term 'Just Society', Liam Cosgrave regularly used the title of the manifesto in his speeches, often saving it for the last line for ultimate effect. His closing words at the final Fine Gael rally at the GPO advised that 'by not wasting your vote on any other party you, the voters, will ensure that Fine Gael gets a decisive mandate to implement progressive reforms and wins through to a "Just Society"'. However, nowhere could the party's policies be better identified than in those speeches made by Michael Sweetman, whose contributions were laced with the language of the Just Society.

In Cabra, Finglas, Ballymun, Phibsboro and other parts of the Dublin North West constituency, he spoke on the subjects of rates, community work, social reform, the Irish language, and local government. His speeches had a dual emphasis on the individual and communities. Himself a statistic of emigration in the 1950s, Michael Sweetman believed in seeing beyond numbers to real people. 'The community is . . . not a set of statistics', he told one audience in Finglas. This comment was in reference to the targets set in the Fianna Fáil government's programme for economic reform. As he further explained, 'it is time we recognised that social reform and social progress are not luxuries

3 *Young tigers and mongrel foxes: A life in politics* (Dublin 2005)

which we must wait for until economic development has reached a certain point'. Fine Gael, he contended elsewhere, would set a new standard in Irish politics that would deliver significant reform, and an air of hopefulness that reflected his own aspirations pervaded his speeches. In Cabra, he spoke of the need for recreational facilities— including playgrounds, youth clubs and community centres—for young people. In Finglas, he argued that the system of rates, which was 'antiquated and unjust', should be abolished as soon as possible. 'It is completely wrong that people should have to pay the same rates whether they are millionaires or old age pensioners', he stated. And in Ballymun he lamented the general contempt for the Irish language. Fine Gael in government would abolish the compulsory Irish criteria for the Intermediate and Leaving Certificate examinations and as a requirement for public service. But the party would also offer incentives to speak and study the language for those who were enthusiastic about it. With a first preference count of 2,180 votes, Michael Sweetman was the second strongest performer of the four Fine Gael candidates in the constituency. However, Dublin North West did not traditionally yield more than one seat for the party and with only 165 votes between him and his running mate Hugh Byrne he was eliminated after the seventh count. The bulk of his transfers subsequently went to Byrne who took the only Fine Gael seat.

The themes in his speeches for the general election were to be repeated in his campaign for that year's Seanad election for which he unsuccessfully stood on the agricultural panel. In his election manifesto he spoke of the necessity for tackling urgent social problems and advocated 'comprehensive reform of our antiquated and class-ridden health and social welfare systems to bring them into line with modern social thinking'. He also advocated reform of the education system and a new drive to reverse the steady disintegration of the rural community, particularly in the west.

His ideas on a just society were not limited to politics in the Republic. Michael Sweetman's views on Northern Ireland and the EEC— discussed more fully elsewhere in this book—were also informed by Just Society thinking. In a draft speech prepared for Liam Cosgrave, he argued that 'the achieving of a just society should be the priority of politicians on both sides of the border. That means making it possible for every Irish person whether in the North or in the South to have decent secure employment, decent living conditions, and fair impartial democratic government'. His concern for a more fair society could be seen in a memorandum to Cosgrave on the benefits of joining the European Community. He pointed out that the cost of living would inevitably rise, but that the increase should not be imposed on those whose incomes and standard of living were already low. He went on to suggest that the money which the government would save once it was relieved of the financial burden of subsidising farmers could be used to compensate people on lower incomes for whatever increases would occur in the cost of living.

Mention has already been made of internal tensions and amateur organisation, but there was a further reason why Fine Gael remained on the opposition benches throughout the 1960s. Labour had resisted the concept of coalition in 1965 and 1969, which greatly diminished Fine Gael's prospects of entering government. As Brendan Corish put it in 1969, 'We will not give the kiss of life to Fine Gael'. However, after that year's bruising election campaign, the party finally abandoned its opposition to coalition at a conference in December the following year. Consequently, Labour and Fine Gael stood on a joint platform for the 1973 election and, almost ten years after Costello first formulated his Just Society policies, the two parties issued a joint programme that bore a striking resemblance to the 1965 manifesto. The advancement of the progressive wing of Fine Gael further continued under the leadership of Garret FitzGerald during his terms in office in the 1980s. However, many of the aims of the Just Society promoted by Declan Costello and supported by people like Michael Sweetman remained unsatisfied. The attempt to shift Fine Gael more to the left also created a lingering identity crisis, with which the party has struggled to come to terms.

Michael Sweetman's commitment to changing Irish society and improving the lives of the less well-off is clearly identifiable across the pages of articles, newspaper letters, speeches and statements that he penned. Although backroom staff are rarely seen or heard, he made an important contribution to the formulation of a policy, which although largely unrealised, offered a blueprint for a new Ireland, and he was an active participant in a debate that proved to be an important turning point in Irish political discourse.

Remembering Michael
and missing him

Vincent Browne*

I tell a story about Garret FitzGerald and Michael which I hope
Garret's family won't mind me putting in print. Were Michael
around he would laugh and laugh at the recollection of the event I
describe, as he did then.

I was editor of a magazine, *Nusight*, in 1969/70. It had been a student publication published by the Union of Students of Ireland (USI)
but by the time I became editor in August 1969 it had become a national current affairs magazine. Gordon Colleary, then chairman of
USIT (the travel company associated with USI), was the person who
involved me in *Nusight*. Others involved were Kevin Myers (then very
much on the left politically), John Feeney, who was killed with several
other journalists, in the 'Beaujolais' aircraft crash in November 1984 (it
was a public relations enterprise to publicise the wine), John Kelleher,
later programme controller of RTÉ and later still film censor, Declan Burke Kennedy, later with *The Irish Times*, Anna Boylan, now
co-director of A. & A. Farmar, publishers, and Cecily O'Toole, later
the mainstay of *Magill*.

Michael and Garret wrote anonymously for *Nusight* (I had the
idea at the time writers and reporters should not have by-lines—quite
daft!). Neither was ever paid. I remember Garret turning up at the
printers in Clonskeagh to proof read. We did some good stuff then,
mainly on Northern Ireland, where the conflict had started in 1968.
We suddenly got a huge circulation boost—from about 5,000 copies
a month to over 30,000 a month with a special issue on events in the
North in August 1969 that included spectacular photographs—but,
as Garret used to recall, we were losing money on every copy sold

* Vincent Browne is a print and broadcast journalist, and a part-time barrister. He
is a columnist with *The Irish Times* and the *Sunday Business Post* and presenter of
Tonight with Vincent Browne on TV3.

because the cover price was too low.

We ran out of money but because the venture had become popular so quickly I was confident I could get investment. One of the people who used to write for *Nusight* at the time was Dorine Reihill, who knew lots of rich people. She persuaded a group of these to invest £20,000 in *Nusight*, a huge sum in 1970. The group wanted to have a meeting with me before handing over the cash. I was a little intimidated by the prospect of having to smooth-talk these high-flyers, so I got Michael and Garret to come along.

We met in the splendid boardroom of USI in a magnificent Georgian building on Harcourt Street—I have no idea why USI had such a grand head office at the time. Dorine's cohort came into the room, led by a formidable character, Noel Griffin, then head of Waterford Glass and very much of the Fianna Fáil persuasion (affliction?). They sat at the head of the table with Garret, Michael and myself towards the far end, Garret and I on one side and Michael across from us.

Almost immediately Garret got into an argument with Noel Griffin—about what I now don't recall—but certainly it had nothing at all to do with the business at hand. The argument grew more and more hot-tempered. I pleadingly muttered to Garret to get him to stop. Michael was rolling his eyes at the other side of the table. Michael was very good at rolling his eyes and knew it. It was one of his few conceits.

The inevitable happened. Noel Griffin said he was not going to be involved in any enterprise that was associated with (expletive deleted). The would-be investors rose and left. Garret, Michael and I sat there silent for a few seconds, until Garret said: 'We're better off without that lot'. Michael and I broke into uncontrollable laughter. Garret did a perfect imitation of his indignant self, which prolonged our uncontrollable laughter, tears streaming down our faces. We went across the road to a small hotel with a tiny bar, the Harcourt Hotel. Garret had a gin and tonic which perfected his imitation of himself. *Nusight* was down the drain. Michael and I laughed and laughed.

In connection with this book I visited Garret sometime last autumn. We thought we might write a joint memoir of Michael. Garret started to tell how he had met Michael at a conference in Copenhagen that had something to do with women's hosiery. I was curious about this and asked Garret to explain. Garret had been working with the Committee for Industrial Organisation, which was established in the early 1960s to help prepare Irish industry for free trade and, ultimately, membership of the EEC, and he had become the coordinator (or some such) for the hosiery sector. Michael was working for the Confederation of Irish Industry (CII), a precursor of IBEC. Michael and Garret were in Copenhagen on business.

At our meeting last autumn, Garret diverted to talk about how he had become an expert on women's stockings and how he had been dismissed as the coordinator of the group looking at women's stockings for a reason he couldn't remember. Garret's imitation of himself in telling about this was achingly funny and we both started to laugh and laugh, again tears running down our faces. I am sure I have got the bit about the women's stockings wrong in some detail, for I was more transfixed on Garret's imitation of himself than I was on the stockings. I thought how Michael would have laughed and laughed had he been there. I can see the laugh, with head turned back, laughing without reserve. Of countless meetings I have had with Garret down the years that must have been the most enjoyable for us both and it was so appropriate Michael was there with us in spirit.

Although I knew Michael for only a few years, I missed him a lot for maybe twenty years after his death. Often I would want to talk to him about something, sometimes personal, usually something to do with politics or journalism, and then realise he was not there anymore. I wondered why I had felt a gulf in my life because of his absence, having known him so briefly. I think it was because I would trust Michael completely, trust his judgement but also trust he would give advice untainted by any personal interest or agenda. I am sure that many others felt the same about him and I felt so sorry at the time of his death and long afterwards that he was not around for years and years to give himself fully, without reserve, to his children, which of course he did until that awful crash.

He was quite daft. He used to make his own beer and wine and when I used to go around to his and Barbara's home when they were in Foxrock, I used to get this beer and wine and I hated both. Awful. And he was so proud of them. Not at all deterred on being told they were vile. I really do recall him, dressed in a three-piece, blueish, slightly speckled suit, digging in the back garden at that Foxrock home, holding a book. I know it is implausible a person would hold an open book in one hand and still dig with a spade but that is my recollection and it fits with his personality and abstractness.

Michael had no vices I knew of and, unlike most people without vices, he had no annoying virtues that I knew of. He was calm, measured, un-judgemental, funny, very clever, open-minded. No preciousness, no pomposity, no ego.

It must have been during the 1966 Presidential campaign of Tom O'Higgins that I got to know him, although I have no specific memory of meeting him then. Michael wrote the major speeches for that Presidential campaign and commenced a change in our political culture that later made this society more inclusive and contributed to the consensus that underpinned the Good Friday Agreement of some thirty-two years later.

Michael was not a socialist—after all he worked for the CII. And the success of the political thrust he brought to that Presidential campaign in 1966 in part diverted Fine Gael from the Just Society line, which Declan Costello had brought to a very unwilling Fine Gael some years previously. I never discussed this explicitly with Michael, but I think his disposition would have been to have given equality a greater prominence than Garret later did—Declan Costello had written in the introduction to *Towards a Just Society* in 1965 that politics is about giving reality to two concepts: liberty and equality. Fine Gael, influenced by Garret, went the liberty way but not much the equality way. I know Declan was disappointed by this. Michael, had he lived, might well have followed a different line.

This might seem implausible to people now—after all Michael was from a privileged background, he worked for a business organisation, and he was drawn towards the most conservative party in the state. But that overlooks his open-mindedness, his intellectual honesty, his instinctual generosity and the absence of any self-interest in his thought process.

He was a lovely man. And it is such such a pity that he wasn't around for decades and decades longer, for Barbara of course, for their children of course, for us his friends of course, but also for the country.

He would be appalled by what has happened over the last few years and I can envisage what his response would have been: to take out that awkward fountain pen and begin to make notes in black ink, while delicately stroking his combed hair with his left hand, smiling ruefully.

I still miss him.

A formative influence

Peter Sutherland*

Although my direct contacts with Michael Sweetman were very limited he represented values and a political position that influenced me greatly in the late 1960s and early 1970s, and opinions that were already in formation in my generation.

During this time Michael was an iconic figure for the small and disparate groups of Fine Gael members who were looking for a new dynamic. Some of us in Dún Laoghaire-Rathdown constituency formed a group (chaired by John Morgan and including Peter Shanley, the nephew of Tom O'Higgins) inspired by the thinking represented for us by Michael Sweetman. Membership of the European Community and the Just Society policies were the essential motivating ideas for many of us in those days, just as they were for him.

Michael is described in the *Dictionary of Irish Biography* as 'one of the progenitors of the Just Society policy' and his connection with Declan Costello was well known. When he stood for election in the late 1960s many of us canvassed for him in Dublin North West. His failure to win a seat (when he was beaten by just 160 votes) was keenly felt by the younger generation of Fine Gaelers in particular. We were fearful that we had lost Declan Costello too. He previously held the seat in Dublin North West but then stood down although it was to transpire that he would stand again in Dublin South West in 1973. Michael's belief in European integration, and his experience of living abroad in England and Canada, had marked him as an internationalist far removed from the insularity of much of Irish politics. His support for the Just Society suggested a direction for the policies of Fine Gael very different from the conservatism that had seemed endemic

* Peter Sutherland was Appointed Attorney General in 1981, age 34. In 1985 he was appointed to the European Commission. He was Director General of the World Trade Organization from 1993 to 1995. He is non-executive chairman of Goldman Sachs International.

in the party. The Central Branch of Fine Gael seemed to me an almost mythical source for modernisation. Although I never attended a meeting, and know very little in reality about it, I know that Michael was a central figure there.

Michael lost out in his general election bid to another Fine Gael candidate Dr Hugh Byrne who was a local GP. As I was to learn in the 1973 election, Hugh Byrne was a doughty political warrior. After Michael's untimely death I was asked to stand in Dublin North West. At this time I had been trying to help Declan Costello in his attempt to win a Fine Gael seat in Dublin South West (which I think was the only constituency in the country where we had no representative). I was the beneficiary of the cadre of supporters of both Declan and Michael in the constituency when I ran unsuccessfully in Dublin North West. I still remember the respect for Michael that I encountered everywhere and I feel proud to have temporarily inherited his mantle. Like him, but perhaps with a less dignified and more acrimonious campaign, I also lost to Dr Hugh Byrne.

A unique man

Christopher Sweetman

Our father was a unique man.

Not because he was our father, obviously that made him unique to us, but because he was a person who thought for himself. In those times in Ireland, the 1960s that I remember and the 1940s and 1950s we read about in school, thinking for yourself was not that common.

Dad was into health food. He brought back muesli from Brussels, the car dashboard always had home-grown apples rolling around, and we were not allowed to eat certain foods—ice pops—too chemical; or to chew gum—bad for the stomach. I do remember negotiating to be able to chew some one time until the sugar was gone.

He wore an old police uniform to go to work on his fruit farm on Saturdays and came back to the car laughing from the Garda station in Athboy because the lads thought he was some kind of runaway cop.

I walked out of Mass with him in support of his protest at some letter or sermon or other. We walked around for a few minutes and then went back to catch the end of the service.

In his way he was traditional. In Donegal we men went off on fishing trips while the women stayed home. All-day fishing trips, a day full of adventure for Patrick and me with uncles, grandfather and whoever else was around. We also had regular Sunday walks, out on Killiney beach or around Dalkey.

We saw Dad on television, something we normally didn't watch because we didn't have one. He looked very smart and sure of himself and his ideas.

We made beer and wine and drank it and laughed a lot. As kids we were given a drop in a glass of water so we could join in.

He was a complete man, our father, complete because, being himself, he could not but be.

The Portsalon conferences[1]

Paddy Harte[*]

The road to peace in Northern Ireland has been a long and arduous process. It was achieved over a lengthy period of time through conferences, behind-the-scene meetings, risks and concessions by both individuals and groups, and a series of settlements. Living in, and having represented the border constituency of Donegal, I have been a close observer of the developments, and I too have played my part in helping to effect change. The pre-Peace Agreement Portsalon conferences of the 1970s were important forums in opening the lines of communication between the different communities. Michael Sweetman—a bright, intelligent young man with a strong interest in Northern affairs and a commitment to finding a peaceful solution—worked alongside me in organising three of these conferences, which ultimately paved the way for a truce.

I met Michael shortly after Declan Costello declined to seek re-election in the 1969 general election mostly, if not entirely, because of irreconcilable differences he had with Gerard Sweetman, Michael's cousin. Declan, the white hope of Fine Gael in the sixties and the initiator of *A Just Society*, admired Michael and encouraged him to contest the Dáil seat he had occupied. Had he been nominated sooner he would have won that seat, coming within 160 votes of victory.

Michael had a very different political outlook to his cousin who was extremely conservative. When asked was he really a cousin of the National Director of Fine Gael, who exerted power and direction in

---

1 Aspects of this chapter draw on matters discussed more fully in my memoir *Young tigers and mongrel foxes: a life in politics* (Dublin 2005)

* Paddy Harte was born in Lifford, Co. He was elected to Donegal County Council in 1960 and to Dáil Éireann in 1961, where he served until 1997. He held office as Minister of State at the Department of Posts and Telegraphs as well as being Spokesman on Northern Ireland. He was a founder member of the Irish American Partnership and organised the building of the Island of Ireland Peace Park in Messines Ridge, Belgium in 1998.

the party, Michael explained that Gerard Sweetman was a first cousin of his father which made him a first cousin once removed, and the farther removed the better! Michael, with Garret FitzGerald and Richard Burke, was part of an ad hoc committee organised by me which produced a party document in September 1969 and gave direction to the peaceful way forward in Ireland North and South.

Through the Taoiseach, Jack Lynch, I was given access to private money to fund a series of weekend conferences at the Portsalon Hotel, Co. Donegal, in early 1972. While no limit was set on the finance available and all receipted expenses would be reimbursed, I was informed that the Taoiseach's name was not to be used in association with the project. Although I informed Liam Cosgrave, my party leader, of my intentions, he would also have been briefed, out of a sense of duty, by Michael Sweetman who served as a scriptwriter to Cosgrave.

On Sunday, 11 June 1972, we met the leaders of 'Women Together', a cross-community group, to finalise the details of a conference scheduled for the following weekend, 16–18 June. Those in attendance had travelled from Coleraine, Bangor, Ballymena, Lurgan, Dungannon, Downpatrick and the suburbs of Belfast. The conference was to be attended solely by women from both communities. An invitation was extended to ten individuals who displayed clear leadership abilities. In turn each of these delegates would invite ten other women. When all 110 attendees were gathered, they were to be subsequently divided into groups of ten to discuss an agreed agenda dealing with the Northern conflict.

On the conclusion of the preliminary meeting, Michael Sweetman and I went our separate ways; he departed for Dublin and I returned to Donegal. That evening a serious gun battle occurred in the Oldpark area of Belfast near where we had met the Women Together members. In a tit-for-tat attack, two Catholic youths and a Protestant woman were shot dead; a soldier also lost his life. The local newspapers reported that twelve people needed medical attention for gunshot wounds.

Street violence had spread to the suburbs of middle-class Belfast, and on the Monday I received a telephone call from the woman in whose home we had had our meeting the previous day. She told me that a number of the women, because of the indiscriminate shootings on the Sunday evening, had changed their minds about attending the conference. By Thursday evening only 40 of the 110 places remained filled. Consequently Michael and I took the decision to postpone the event. Michael, who also had an interest in European affairs, had been due to attend a meeting in Brussels on Monday 19 June, but he had asked to be excused because the Portsalon conference was scheduled for the preceding weekend, his interest in Northern affairs taking precedence. However, with the conference now rescheduled, he decided to fulfil the Brussels engagement.

On the evening of Sunday, 18 June, I was in Rathmullan, Co. Donegal, a very short distance from Portsalon, when Jim Deeney of The Pier Hotel enquired, 'did you know Michael Sweetman?' 'Jim', I asked, 'why have you put the question like that?' 'Because he was killed in that plane crash at London airport this evening,' he replied. Michael Sweetman was thirty-six years old when he died alongside eleven other leading Irish businessmen. Before his death he had been writing a reply to the New Ulster Movement. *The Common Name of Irishman* was published posthumously by his friends, including myself, at the request of his widow, Barbara.

Later I thought that if there had been no gun battle in the normally quiet suburbs of Belfast, our plans to proceed with the Portsalon conference would not have been altered and Michael Sweetman would still be alive. It could be said that he too lost his life because of the Northern violence. Three members of Women Together attended the funeral at St Francis Xavier Church, Gardiner Street in Dublin where his uncle, Fr Michael Sweetman, celebrated the Requiem Mass.

In the aftermath of Michael Sweetman's death, I persisted with the idea of cross-community conferences. On Friday, 21 July 1972, I travelled alone to Belfast to meet the women from the organisation at the Regency Hotel to renew our efforts. The aim of the meeting was to establish if the women were still interested in proceeding. I was told that, while they would welcome being involved in anything that would lead to peace, the continuing violence was making them cautious. The meeting was brief, and we agreed to reconvene in September or October. Later that day as I was walking along Great Victoria Street, I thought I heard the sound of bombs exploding. I was right. The violence was ferocious and savage on that day, which later came to be known as Bloody Friday. The year 1972 was the single most bloody and violent year of the Northern troubles, and the growing violence thwarted any further attempts to organise a Women Together conference for that year.

In February 1973, Jack Lynch dissolved the nineteenth Dáil and in the subsequent election, Liam Cosgrave and Fine Gael, along with the Labour Party, formed a new coalition government. I retained my seat for Donegal North East and found that Dáil and constituency matters demanded more of my time; the organisation of another Portsalon conference was put on the long finger. As I have discussed in *Young Tigers and Mongrel Foxes*, Cosgrave did not have the same interest in continuing the Portsalon programme. In fairness, the situation in Northern Ireland in 1973 was changing. There was a bigger picture to be looked at as all political parties geared up for local elections in May and Assembly elections in June; the White Paper on Constitutional Proposals—produced in March—and the future of Northern Ireland held centre stage.

In December 1973, a conference was convened in Berkshire at which representatives of the British and Irish governments, as well as those of the parties that favoured power-sharing in the North, participated. The outcome was a document which became known as the Sunningdale Agreement. It was signed on 6 December 1973 and it came into effect in Northern Ireland on New Year's Day, 1974.

The signing of the Agreement did not meet with popular approval in Protestant Belfast, and on 10 December Loyalist paramilitaries, including members of the UDA and UVF, issued statements opposing it. Later I got to know many of the leaders of the Loyalist groups and was told that they had taken action because of the lack of political leadership. It is now generally believed that the section dealing with the Council of Ireland was the only part of what could be described as a reasonably fair Agreement that frightened the masses of the Protestant people. Once the Council of Ireland was removed, the Loyalist paramilitaries lost popular support. But before that happened, the Ulster Unionist Council—the authority within the Unionist Party—had its say.

A total of 801 delegates voted on the terms of Sunningdale, put before them by the Unionist leader, Brian Faulkner. It was rejected by a margin of 50 votes, or 6 per cent. A good number of delegates voted against the Agreement because they did not fully understand its terms and because they wanted to frighten Faulkner. They did not all, however, mean for him to be sacked. A settlement had been so near, and yet so far.

When Faulkner lost he was replaced by Harry West, whom I knew well. In time he told me how he had voted against and privately regretted the badly handled presentation of the Agreement. I got to know West a lot better as time and common concern brought us together, and it is only right that I should put on record that he was not a bitter, hard-line politician. He was quite friendly, and a pleasure to know and speak with. He often visited Donegal and I had the pleasure of visiting his home in Enniskillen. He did not see the Agreement as I saw it, but time and effort, I believe, would have settled that. Our views were not that different. I solemnly believe that if the mix had been right, he would have supported an agreed Ireland.

On 14 May 1974, the Ulster Workers' Council issued a call for a general strike, which began the next day. It is very difficult to see how it could have been averted. Bill Craig, MP and a prominent Unionist leader, asked in September 1971:

> 'Does the South realise the power the unionist people have in this part of Ireland? We could cut off the electricity from almost every Catholic home; we could cut off water supply; reverse the pumps in the sewerage systems; refuse to supply petrol and diesel to Catholics. We control telephones, radio and television stations. Without firing a shot we could close this place down and tell you all to go away unless all Catholics became like us. That power is in our hands, and when you go back to Dublin tell them what I said.'

This was the same Bill Craig who told the right-wing Monday Club in October 1972 that he could mobilise 80,000 men to oppose the British government. 'We are prepared to come out and shoot and kill. Let us put the bluff aside. I am prepared to kill and those behind me will have my full support.' He was foretelling what happened during the Ulster Workers' strike and maybe, just maybe, if that nettle had been grasped, better understood and acted upon before militants had taken up an entrenched position, the history of the period might not have been so violent. It is very wrong to think that all Protestants think alike. I always believed the Protestant community was as divided as the Catholics. Participants who became involved in the Portsalon conferences were solid, good thinking individuals and cross-community groups whose only agenda was peace. Many since then have expressed the opinion that I should have been getting greater support from party leaders in Dublin. More conferences like Portsalon should

[84]

have been held in venues north and south of the Border, as well as in Scotland, Wales and England.

The Ulster Workers' strike happened because the Sunningdale agreement had been badly understood. It would be unfair to blame those who opposed it for its failure because, I believe, by the laws of average, half of the Protestant people accepted it. The concept in itself was good, but it was taken for granted by those who believed. What Michael Sweetman and I tried to develop was the embryo of a better way forward, but men of peace in government in Dublin could not recognise this.

I am confident that if the coalminers' strike, which resulted in a general election in Britain and Northern Ireland, had not happened, the Northern community would have worked its way through the difficulties of the Agreement as they would eventually do, with time and effort, twenty-five years later in the form of the Good Friday Agreement. That strike was far from the minds of voters in Northern Ireland and Arthur Scargill, leader of the coal miners' union, was no more than a name. Nonetheless, Scargill unintentionally wrecked the Sunningdale Agreement, which I doubt he knew existed. Scargill had the power to pull down the British government and the resulting general election in Northern Ireland presented the anti-Agreement Unionists with an opportunity to treat the election as a referendum 'for' or 'against' Sunningdale. Their leadership united and decided to form a new group. The United Ulster Unionist Council brought together the Ulster Unionists, Vanguard Unionist and Democratic Unionist parties which agreed not to oppose one another but to unite against Sunningdale. In contrast, the pro-Agreement parties were disjointed, with the consequence that eleven of the twelve anti-Agreement MPs were elected with larger majorities than was normal. Gerry Fitt was the only pro-Agreement candidate to be elected when he defeated a DUP member by 2,000 votes.

Within a month of Sunningdale being defeated, there were calls for a fresh election from the Ulster Workers Council, a new organisation. The calls had been prompted by the threat of industrial action from the United Ulster Unionist Council, which was demanding a vote. On the Unionist side, the battle had begun between the politicians of the United Ulster Unionist Council and the Loyalist working class grouping of the Ulster Workers Council. The North was on the road to a general strike and when the government agreed to put the army in charge of filling stations, the future looked bleak.

In June 1974 the Loyalists held a weekend conference which I could have attended because of my contacts through the Portsalon conferences, but people would have recognised me and it was a bridge too far. Shortly afterwards, Republican circles concluded that working-class Protestants were socialist and different to those who led the United Ulster Unionist Council. This had a ring of truth to it. It was an open secret in certain Belfast circles that Loyalist and Republican leaders were in contact with each other. It was also generally believed that Loyalist and Republican paramilitary prisoners in the Maze had common concerns. On a visit to the home of Máire Drumm, vice-president of Provisional Sinn Féin, she openly told me that the Republicans were favourably considering talks with the UDA. Andy Tyrie, leader of that organisation, later confirmed the story.

It was the summer of 1974 before I was buttonholed again on the Portsalon project. This time the proposal was to bring together twenty-five members each of the UDA, UVF, Provisional IRA and Official IRA. The participants would be supervised by ten non-government, professional facilitators: surgeon John Robb, later nominated to Seanad Éireann; Professor Howell Griffiths, Queen's University, Belfast (QUB); Jim Fitzpatrick, chairman, the *Irish News*; Professor Tom Lovett, QUB; Tony Spencer, QUB; Joe Mulvenna, NI Community Workers Council; Andy Robinson, commander, UDA, Derry; Professor Stanley Worrell, headmaster, Instonian College, Belfast; R. J. Spjut, QUB; and Charlie Hill QC, Belfast. Joe Camplisson acted as co-ordinator.

It was an ambitious programme. The weekend of 13–15 September 1974 was agreed and I brought the proposal to Liam Cosgrave. Cosgrave was not in the habit of dealing with Loyalist or Republican terrorists, but he listened to me and without reference to any other minister or adviser, he agreed so long as I understood that I was not representing his government. I was on my own, but I could, discreetly, as a Dáil deputy, call on the help of government agencies. Money was coming from both sides of the border and was not an issue.

Like the Women Together programme, the attendees were broken up into groups of ten. No minutes of the various meetings would be kept, but each group would agree on a prepared statement that would summarise the discussion that had taken place. The conference would conclude with a plenary session. I kept a low profile, but was available to assist should I be needed. On the Saturday I was asked to identify one person who was not a participant. I recognised him as a Special Branch officer and quietly asked him to leave. On Sunday, I was talking with Harry Chicken, deputy commander of the UDA, when Séamus Loughran, PR for Sinn Féin, asked me to meet a group of Provisionals led by Máire Drumm. I agreed. A short discussion ensued in which Chicken politely, but bluntly, answered the question, 'will the unionists ever join a united Ireland?', by saying, 'never the way you people are going, but they might be persuaded to consider Paddy Harte's Ireland'.

When I met the group of Provisionals privately, they told me that they were glad they had participated. I told them that, while I was happy they had attended, I took issue with the word 'participate'. 'You did not, as a group, take part. You listened and asked questions, but frankly I was disappointed because I have been listening all my life to Republicans telling me it was time to get everyone around the table to talk and this weekend there were people here wanting to talk and your group listened, but did not talk'. Máire Drumm said that the group did not have the authority to talk, but the next time that a weekend was organised they would be there and have things to say. 'I will hold you to that', I responded as we parted.

The following morning, 16 September 1974, Judge Rory Conaghan and Magistrate Martin McBirney were shot dead in Belfast as they answered the front door of their respective homes. Loyalists blamed the IRA for the killings. 'What is the point of meeting them on Sunday when they murder two judges on Monday?', Andy Tyrie asked. Máire Drumm asked me to meet her. She told me she had no knowledge of who had carried out the shootings and if she ever got to know, she would have things to say about the matter. She asked me to continue with the Portsalon programme.

Loyalists retaliated and street violence increased in a 'tit-for-tat' campaign, leaving a trail of death and destruction across Northern Ireland and Britain. Westminster enacted the Prevention of Terrorism Act, 1974, making it possible to arrest and detain suspects without trial. Such legislation was unprecedented in peacetime, but justified nonetheless. In the days preceding its introduction, nineteen people were killed and 182 injured by IRA bombs in Birmingham.

I gave Liam Cosgrave a report on the conference and though I knew he admired what I had achieved, he never wanted to be associated with paramilitaries and I never approached him again. It was not his forte. He did not know if he should encourage me to continue the programme as a non-governmental organisation or dissuade me. Looking back and comparing Liam Cosgrave's attitude with Jack Lynch's, I find myself drawing a conclusion that, regrettably, would not be favourable to my party leader.

I continued to meet people in Belfast and got to know that members of the non-government professional facilitators who had managed the September conference in Portsalon were in contact with leaders of the IRA, but their talks were strictly confidential and I respected that position. Stanley Worrell, with whom I developed a close friendship, played a lead role in keeping in touch with Provisional Sinn Féin members who attended that conference. He helped arrange a meeting with the IRA army council in Feakle, Co. Clare for 10 December 1974, three months after the Portsalon conference.

The Feakle meeting led to a temporary ceasefire in Northern Ireland beginning on 22 December. On 9 February the Provisional IRA declared an indefinite ceasefire that led to the setting up of incident centres throughout Northern Ireland. Manned by Provisional Sinn Féin, their aim was to monitor the ceasefire with British government officials. The centres came to symbolise the truce itself. Ruairí Ó Brádaigh, the president of Provisional Sinn Féin, called them 'the very legs on which the truce stands', while Máire Drumm said they constituted a power base for Sinn Féin. According to the Provisional IRA, the British government agreed to twelve points: the release of 100 detainees within a two or three week period; phasing out of internment within a specific period; the effective withdrawal of the army from barracks, meaning the return of 3,000–4,000 troops to Britain within six months; an end to the system of arrests, screening and large scale searches in Catholic areas; the establishment of incident centres, manned by members of Sinn Féin and connected with an incident room at Stormont with the objective of monitoring the ceasefire; a provision for 'army-to-army' discussions at local level; an end to military check points and road blocks at the edge of Catholic areas; immunity from arrest for specified persons; firearm licences for specified persons; no immediate attempts to introduce the RUC or UDR into Catholic areas; a formal ceasefire agreement to be drawn up by the British; and further talks to take place between IRA leaders and senior British representatives.

The relationship between the British government and the IRA during the ceasefire was highly contentious. While the Northern Ireland Office consistently rejected claims that they had done a deal with the Provisionals, when Daithí Ó Conaill, IRA chief of staff, was arrested in Dublin in September and the Gardaí uncovered what appeared to be a copy of the twelve-point peace deal, the British government took the unusual step of officially denying the authenticity of the document. The IRA felt that the negotiations undertaken during the truce would lead to a British withdrawal from Northern Ireland, although they knew that the British could not admit to this publicly.

In a letter to *The Irish Times* on 30 April 1992, Ó Brádaigh set out his view of the period. It is worth quoting at length:

> Resulting from Feakle, a unilateral truce by the Irish Republican Army was declared and observed from December 22, 1974, until January 16, 1975. Following the expiration of this and renewed army activity by both British forces and the IRA, talks were entered into—at the request of the British—for three weeks and the outcome was a bilateral truce on written terms from February 10, with monitoring mechanisms in place.
>
> The republicans were in receipt of a message from the British over the Christmas period that 'HMG wished to devise structures of disengagement from Ireland'.
>
> The bilateral truce lasted until September 22 that year with various near-breaking points along the way. Truce-monitoring meetings and separate political meetings took place right through from February to September between 'HMG representatives' and those of 'the Republican movement', as they variously called themselves.
>
> The representatives offered to deliver a permanent ceasefire in return for a public British declaration that it would quit Ireland by a date to be negotiated. The discussions failed and the bilateral truce failed even though the British secretary of state at the time, Merlyn Rees, admitted afterwards in a letter to the London *Times* in July 1983 that the cabinet sub-committee dealing with Ireland had 'seriously considered' withdrawal.

Ó Brádaigh went on to outline three reasons as to why he felt that the truce had failed:

> (a) the loyalist death squads immediately embarked on the greatest as-

sassination campaign of innocent Catholics up to date (b) the Dublin government indicated to the British that a withdrawal must not be contemplated ('Dublin was becoming increasingly "twitchy" at the continuation of the truce and the talks', the British representative said) and a key republican leader, Dáithí Ó Conaill, was singled out and hunted down by them in early July; and (c) finally in the outcome the British did not deliver on their promise of the previous Christmas.[2]

Some of the Provisionals' twelve points undoubtedly operated. Seven 'incident centres' were set up, security activity in Catholic areas was scaled down, and leading Provisionals were apparently not arrested when identified by the army. In effect, the government acquiesced in the Provisional IRA maintaining a high-profile presence in Catholic areas. Labour politicians and NIO members later claimed that the purpose of the truce had been to divide the Provisional leadership and create conditions that would bring an end to internment. Some observers believe this to be a retrospective rationalisation of the situation.

All of this had resulted from the meeting in Feakle in December 1974. Although Michael Sweetman did not live to witness the ceasefire, the conferences which we had co-organised were an important foundation stone. The outcome at Feakle was arguably the culmination of a process which we had initiated with the Portsalon conferences, to which proper credit has never been given.

2 Letter to the editor, *The Irish Times*, 30 April 1992

Report of Conference at Portsalon Hotel, County Donegal Friday, Saturday and Sunday, 14th, 15th and 16th April 1972

Michael Sweetman

How it came about

As a result of talks between people on both sides of the political spectrum in Northern Ireland it was felt that it could be an advantage to aim at selecting a group of people from a wide area and invite them to spend the weekend together away from the tension of their own environment.

The possibility of finding suitable premises in Northern Ireland was considered but it was felt that Co. Donegal with its close identification with the Northern people could provide the answer. Mr Paddy Harte, TD was given permission to investigate venues. Through the co-operation of Mr E. Hoy of the North Western Tourism Organisation Portsalon Hotel was found to be available and suitable.

Mr Hoy recognised the debt that Donegal people owed the Northern community and also the deep desire Donegal people had to try to help find solutions, and generously agreed to make financial aid available and for this both he and his Board receive our sincere thanks.

Arrangements were then made to select the attendance and twenty people were asked to invite four other people from the area whom they felt would benefit from such a weekend, and final arrangements were made. There was an attendance of 78 people.

The group arrived on Friday night and were welcomed by Most Rev. Dr A. McFeely, Bishop of Raphoe, and Venerable Archdeacon Crooks MA (representing Rev. Dr Peacocke, Bishop of Derry and

Raphoe). Reverend Dr A. Martin, former Moderator of the Presbyterian Church was unavoidably absent and sent his apologies and good wishes. Later a steering group met and appointed eight group leaders and divided the attendance into working groups.

On Saturday the Conference met and the following Agenda was agreed:

10.30 Assemble

10.45 Group meetings

12.15 Report from Group Leaders

1 o'c. Lunch

2.15 Open Forum

4 o'c. Tea

4.15 Ireland and Europe Economic & Social Development North and South followed by questions.

6 o'c. Conclude

7 o'c. Dinner

9 o'c. Social evening.

Other points discussed and agreed to were:

(1) Desirability of a peace conference between Shankill and Falls Road areas to be conducted in private.

(2) Phased withdrawal of army from certain areas as conditions permit.

(3) Meeting of a Shankill Group to be addressed by Michael Sweetman on EEC.

(4) Possibility of the formation of a Council of Ireland to deal with economic and social development on each side of the border with particular reference to border Counties.

Finally it was requested that a list of all those attending should be sent to each person and it was recommended that early contact be made with people living near each other with a view to holding small meetings and increasing members. It was also agreed that the possibility of repeating the Conference on a suitable date should be considered—details to be circulated soon.

Final session

The Group met again on Sunday and discussed the problems on two levels (a) short term (b) long term. On the short term it was felt that for the Catholic community to be successful in their efforts of peace there must be an end to internment and detention. It was pointed out that many people in the Catholic areas wanted peace and would be prepared to work for genuine peace but could not in conscience associate themselves if relatives and close friends were held without trial. The representatives of Catholic areas present stressed that their effort would be successful if an answer to the internment problem could be found. The Protestant representatives also wanted internment without trial ended and recognised that many people interned are most possibly innocent but some could be guilty and the question what would happen the guilty if and when internment ended. The Conference further considered this point and felt that on balance a general pardon should be seriously considered followed by a pledge by all sides publicly to demonstrate for peace. This would allow the politicians an opportunity to meet under Mr Whitelaw to negotiate a peaceful solution. The following Motion was voted on by a show of hands of all present:

'That this Conference favours a general amnesty for political prisoners, detainees and internees both Protestant and Catholic, so that opinions throughout the entire community can be mobilised for peace.'

Three voted against and four abstained.

The weekend was non political and non sectarian but was interdenominational and was aimed at providing an opportunity for people of various views to give expression to them in the hope that bridges would be built between people. It was not aimed at changing a political view. The theme was trust and better understanding.

Michael Sweetman's involvement in the EEC campaign and in Northern Ireland

Dennis Kennedy*

In 1972, when Michael Sweetman died, the Republic of Ireland was faced with two fundamental questions requiring clear and immediate answers:

- Did Ireland's future lie as a small independent state with close economic links to neighbouring countries, or should it opt for sharing its sovereignty—and inevitably diluting it—with other European states within the 'ever closer union' of the European Economic Community?

- How should Ireland—its government, its politicians and its people—react to the upheaval in Northern Ireland and the rapid increase in violence there?

The first question came with a deadline—the referendum on EEC membership on 10 May of that year. The rapid deterioration in the situation in Northern Ireland in 1972 began with Bloody Sunday in Derry and the burning of the British Embassy in Dublin, then the suspension of Stormont, and increasing demands from the nationalist minority for direct help from Dublin. All this meant the second question was just as urgent.

The two questions became intertwined. The common issue was sovereignty—its defence in one context, its assertion in the other. Opposition to EEC membership eventually solidified in the aptly

* Dennis Kennedy has been variously a journalist, a European Commission functionary and a university lecturer. Educated at Queen's University, Belfast, and Trinity College Dublin, he worked as a journalist in Belfast, Dublin, the United States and Ethiopia, ending 17 years with *The Irish Times* in Dublin in 1985 as Deputy Editor. From 1985 to 1991 he was European Commission representative in Belfast.

named Irish Sovereignty Movement, which had a strong Republican/ IRA flavour to it. From that perspective, opposition to EEC membership was as much opposition to an open-ended economic and political alliance with Britain as it was to immersion in an integrating Europe. A No to Europe would be the only way to defend Irish sovereignty.

In the North the vigorous civil rights agitation of the late 1960s had degenerated into widespread sectarian violence. An increasingly well-organised and well-armed IRA had re-emerged and was challenging British sovereignty in arms and reasserting the Irish nationalist sovereignty over the whole island which had been proclaimed in 1916 (and was still asserted in the Irish Constitution).

Should the Government revert to a pre-Lemass anti-partitionism, claiming that partition was the problem, and the only way to solve it was by Britain withdrawing from Northern Ireland, or at least making a declaration of intent in that direction? Should Dublin give aid and support to those using arms inside Northern Ireland, by sending the forces of the state across the border, as some were apparently contemplating, or by secretly funding the IRA on the grounds that it was defending a beleaguered minority?

Many who would not have countenanced such behaviour by a modern democratic state were still ambivalent about the IRA, willing, privately, to give financial aid to groups linked to it, and in public unwilling to be explicit in condemnation of the use of armed force.

The openly Republican supporters of the IRA campaign were also the leading opponents of the plan to take Ireland into the EEC. By no means everyone opposing entry was also an IRA supporter, but the overlap was undeniable, and the public argument as it developed before the May vote was increasingly about sovereignty.

When the 10 May referendum delivered a massive 5 to 1 majority for EEC membership, in an almost 71 per cent poll—a turn-out in a referendum never since repeated—it seemed that the Irish people had given an unequivocal Yes to the EEC and an equally unequivocal No to the IRA and extremist physical force nationalism.

When, the following February, Fianna Fáil lost power to a coalition led by the more enthusiastically pro-Europe Fine Gael and a Labour Party resolutely opposed to the use of armed force, the significance of the referendum vote seemed to be confirmed. Ireland rapidly became recognised as one of the most committed members of the EEC, and hopes soared of a negotiated, peaceful, settlement in Northern Ireland which would consign the IRA finally to history, and sideline the no-sayers of intransigent Unionism.

How then, three or four decades later, do we find Ireland becoming the main obstacle to progress and reform in the EU, rejecting, by referendum, first the Nice Treaty and then, in 2008, the Lisbon Treaty, thereby single-handedly holding up the implementation of essential reforms for more than a year?

How, too, if violence in pursuit of political goals was so over-whelmingly rejected in 1972, did another 3,300 people die in terrorist related violence *after* the May 1972 vote, with the Provisional IRA in the lead? And how could it be that almost four decades later, republican terrorists were still killing people in Northern Ireland?

Even more disquieting, despite governments in London and Dublin repeatedly pledging their determination to defeat the terrorists, the leaders of the main terrorist campaign, still proudly defending the rightness of their terrorist deeds, are now in government in Belfast, as are their colleagues, the followers of Ian Paisley, the man deemed by many to have made the biggest individual contribution to fomenting sectarian hatred and division within Northern Ireland.

The euphoria surrounding the Belfast Agreement, and its survival for more than a decade of stuttering efforts at implementation, have helped camouflage these grave contradictions in the 1998 'settlement', and also the growing evidence of the inefficiency of its cumbersome mechanisms.

The substantial reduction in violence, the appearance if not the reality of coalition power-sharing government and the general air of normality and economic progress are all plus factors to be welcomed. They leave some hope, for irrepressible optimists, that if enough people think, for long enough, that the problem has been solved, it will be. If factions with totally contradictory long-range goals, and long-nurtured hatreds of each other, are obliged to work together within imposed structures for long enough, then perhaps they will forget their conflicting aims and hatreds and just get on with living together. But within what political framework can such living together be accommodated on a long-term basis?

So is the general optimism of today any more soundly based than that of the first half of 1972? Probably not.

The European Union

The decision to join the EEC in 1972 was not, though it may have seemed it at the time, a historic turning point in Ireland's view of itself as an independent state. The idealistic isolationism of de Valera had not survived the post-war era. By the 1960s Irish troops were active participants in UN peace-keeping operations, Ireland had applied, unsuccessfully, for EEC membership in 1961, and the Anglo-Irish Free Trade Agreement of 1965 acknowledged and formalised Ireland's enormous dependence on trade with the United Kingdom. The 1972 referendum vote was popular endorsement of a well-established trend.

While the Irish people generally took pleasure in their new European status, and professed their support for European membership, they were not transformed from Irish nationalists into European integrationists. One of the most frequently voiced arguments for joining the EEC was an essentially nationalist one—it would at last free Ireland from the grip of her unbalanced bi-lateral dependence on Britain. Britain and Ireland would be equals at the European table.

That argument was economic as well as political, and in that was eminently sensible, but it was based more on justifiable self-interest than on commitment to European integration. The very strong farming lobby in favour of EEC membership was similarly grounded in the immediate and foreseeable needs of the farming community.

Nevertheless, Ireland was perceived as among the most positive member states of the European Economic Community, later the European Union, and Eurobarometer[1] polls regularly showed the Irish as not just topping the list of those who felt their country had benefited from membership, but also as being among the most enthusiastic supporters of the process of European integration. In a 1999 Eurobarometer survey, Ireland was the member state most supportive of EU membership, and the country surest that it had benefited from EU membership.

1 Eurobarometer is the twice yearly survey of public opinion across the EU produced since 1973 by the European Commission.

But responses to other questions showed that Irish people's enthusiasm for all things European was waning. While they still felt that progress towards integration should go further, they were not among the leading advocates of such progress.

Still, none of this prepared the politicians or the people for the shock defeat of the Nice Treaty referendum in June 2001, a result which made Ireland no longer the favourite son but the problem child of Europe. Poor political leadership, general indifference and a very small poll were blamed for the defeat, but it was that most nationalistic of preoccupations, Irish neutrality, which probably counted most. A second attempt at the hurdle after a soothing declaration on neutrality from the EU, saw the Nice Treaty endorsed in the referendum of October 2002.

Five years later, in 2007, the Irish people were affirming in another survey how well they thought of the EU—74 per cent said Irish membership was a good thing (only two other countries were more positive) and a whopping 87 per cent said Ireland had benefited from membership, more than in any other member state. But they were not at all keen to identify themselves as 'European' or EU citizens, rather than simply, and exclusively, Irish. And they were also preparing to reject the Lisbon Treaty in the referendum of June 2008.

The sharply contested campaign for Lisbon, and the re-run referendum in October 2009, highlighted concern for national interest narrowly, and mistakenly, defined. Neutrality was raised again, as was the preservation of Ireland's (unfair) advantage over fellow member states in the matter of company taxation, and the question of what was incorrectly termed 'Ireland's Commissioner'. In fact, the argument between the political establishment and the No camp in both referendums was somewhat unreal, for the Government and its fellow Yes men were as anxious as anyone else to preserve neutrality, the tax advantage and the 'Irish' Commissioner.

Why was it deemed so important for Ireland to retain its right to nominate a member of the European Commission? Had it more to do with national pride than with national interest?

When the EEC was created, it was laid down that the Commission must include a national from each member state, so each member state had the right to nominate one national to the Commission—just to nominate, appointing was the task of the Council of Ministers. The thinking behind this was not to ensure national representation on the Commission—Commissioners had to be completely independent of national governments—but to bring to the Commission knowledge and understanding of each state, and also to ensure that the general public in each state would have a sense of participation in the central institution of the union.

Even if the system had worked as envisaged, the number of member states had multiplied by the time of the Nice Treaty to the extent that the Commission was unwieldy in size, and sectoral responsibilities had to be sub-divided, even invented, to give every member a portfolio.

But the system had not worked well. Commissioners often saw themselves, and were seen as, 'representatives' of their own state. Commissioners from many states were often nominated less because of their personal abilities and commitment to the European idea, than for party loyalty and the convenience of the party in power. Not a few were lame ducks, under-performing and weakening the authority of the Commission.

Commissioners and their *cabinets* also became drivers of national interest within the Commission, seeing as one of their main tasks the advancement of their fellow nationals in its professional ranks. Nationality became a more vital qualification than ability for promotion to the higher echelons, and a further source of weakness in the Commission.

This weakening of the Commission suited those member states, mostly the larger ones, who from the outset had worked to tilt the balance of power within the European institutions away from the supranational Commission and towards the member states. Over the years the regular summits of heads of government have eroded the Commission's leadership role in the evolution of the EU.

By the time of the Lisbon Treaty, Ireland had become the most vocal defender of the right of every member state to nominate one of its own nationals to the post of Commissioner, and therefore ensure an ever larger, and weaker, Commission. Yet the real interests of a small member state should surely be to strengthen the Commission, not to weaken it—such had been Ireland's professed approach since entry in 1973. So a move to ensure a more efficient Commission was resolutely, and successfully, opposed by Ireland.

The extent to which Irish governments disregard the independence of the Commission—and therefore weaken it—was illustrated in the spat in 2009 over an appointment to Máire Geoghegan-Quinn's *cabinet* in Brussels. The Taoiseach told the Dáil he saw nothing wrong in 'indicating' to the newly nominated Commissioner that a Senator from one of the Government parties was 'interested' in a job in her cabinet. There was much indignation when the appointment was not forthcoming.[2]

Another blatant case of putting nationalism above real national interest was the insistence on having Irish designated as an official language of the EU in 2007. As a result of the sensible compromise agreement on Irish embodied in the Treaty of Accession, the budget and the mechanisms of the EU had, for more than three decades, been spared the enormous burden of an additional official language which none of the nationals of the country proposing it needed to conduct business, and in which many of them would not have been capable of conducting business. But Irish pride, or the prospect of several hundred jobs for Irish speakers at the EU's expense, took precedence over the efficient and economic working of the EU.

In the two Lisbon referendum campaigns particularly, the strong nationalistic opposition to things European was joined by a more articulate British-style Euroscepticism. It included intellectuals who had been among the sharpest critics of traditional nationalism and Republicanism, but it was itself essentially nationalistic on Lisbon, campaigning on neutrality, and demanding the retention for Ireland of veto rights, tax privileges, and its own Commissioner. It was a new sort of nationalism, but still self-consciously, even arrogantly Irish. It asserted itself more recently in the reaction of some to the 2010 economic rescue package from the International Monetary Fund and the European Central Bank—an ill-tempered threat to bite the helping hand, fuelled by delusions of national greatness and sovereignty.

Northern Ireland

Twenty-six years after 1972, and after thousands more had died in the Troubles in Northern Ireland, the Irish state changed its Constitution to modify its outright claim to the territory of the whole island. There is scant ground for arguing that had this been done in 1972 a single

2 See *The Irish Times*, 24 February 2010.

life would have been saved, but the reluctance to give an inch on the constitutional claim and the niggardly wording of the amendment—diluting rather than deleting the claim—all combined to suggest that neither 1972 nor the intervening years had seen any fundamental rethink on the Northern issue.

The claim to the whole island is implied in the retention of Article 4, which continues to appropriate the name of the island as the name of the state occupying only three quarters of it. The new and rather verbose Articles 2 and 3 link 'the Irish nation' to the whole island and incorporate the aspiration towards unity and the expectation of its accomplishment.

In 1972, the Government, all the main political parties, and the generality of the population were agreed that Irish unification was not only historically and morally right, but was the only way to solve the Northern problem, and also that unification could be achieved only by peaceful means and by agreement, and that Britain could and should facilitate unification by indicating its willingness to withdraw from Northern Ireland.

Today, the Government and all the main political parties, and the generality of the population still think much the same. The commitment to unity by agreement, and by peaceful means only, has been made more explicit, and Britain has, in essence, declared its readiness (perhaps even eagerness) to withdraw as soon as a majority in Northern Ireland tells it to.

But has there been a real re-think on the fundamentals? If anything, today there is no thinking at all—no pondering what will happen if there is no consent to unity, no speculating on what sort of island a united one might be. The political parties still parrot the traditional anti-partition rhetoric, but clearly have other priorities. The people at large certainly have other priorities.

In early 1972, Michael Sweetman, then heading the pro-EEC referendum campaign, but also deeply concerned about the Northern crisis, drafted a pamphlet, which was published shortly after his death under the title *The Common Name of Irishman*. In it he outlined a framework for a settlement in the North which bears a close resemblance to Sunningdale and to the Belfast Agreement, containing all their main institutional and inter-governmental aspects but with the vital difference that power-sharing in a Northern Ireland executive was to be achieved, for an initial period, by any voluntary coalition which could command 75 per cent support in the assembly. It also assumed, wrongly, that the May 1972 referendum had proved conclusively that the cult of physical force had no significant support.

But the originality of *The Common Name of Irishman* lies not in the solution put forward, but in the analysis behind it and the reasons for it. The proposal's sole justification was pragmatic—that it could help the people of the island live in reasonable accord and increased prosperity. It discounted any arguments based on historic injustices, imagined or real. 'History', Michael Sweetman wrote,

> cannot be used to justify a united Ireland. History does not confer 'rights' of the kind implied in traditional nationalist ideology . . . It is the living who have rights to organise their affairs in whatever way suits them best . . . the wrongs of the past do not invalidate the basic rights of the individual today; in this sense the citizen of Northern Ireland has the right today freely to choose his own future within the Northern Ireland framework, even though the establishment of that framework fifty years ago may have been a wrong, even an unjust decision.

The pamphlet questions the very concept of 'the nation'; it is, it says, an abstract idea, and the attempt to give it concrete form in Europe cost the lives of more than fifty million people in two world wars. In a refreshingly Sweetmanish style it declares, with reference to the people of the island,—'the vast majority of us are a mongrel lot, coming in all conceivable colours, shapes and sizes', not classifiable into one, two or any other number of nations.

Having deemed the hysterical Britishness of 'Union-Jack-waving, God-Save-the-Queen Northerners' as more to do with local factionalism than British nationality, the pamphlet then dismisses 'the tricolour-waving, Soldier-Song-singing, decade-of-the-rosary-in-Irish-reciting groups' as reflecting not a love of Ireland or of religion as much as the reassertion of a particular brand of nationalism.

In an article written in April 1972, following the British government's suspension of the Stormont parliament, Michael Sweetman argued that by that action London had swept away a great deal of what was done in Northern Ireland since 1912.

'We, too, have got to go back to 1912 and relinquish a great deal of what has happened since in the South in order that both parts of the country can make a new start,' he wrote, going on to deplore consistent attempts to impose a narrow concept of Irishness involving the primacy of Gaelic culture, the rejection of British strands in Irish traditions, and a particular view of history which made a virtue of fighting against Britain and a vice of defending British rule. 'It is not from that kind of Republicanism with its glorification of violence in the past and its incitement to violence in the present that the new Ireland will come.'[3]

Contained in these two pieces of writing is a prescription for a real rethinking of Irishness, a genuine cultural revolution. The very idea of 'going back to 1912' would still today be anathema not just to Sinn Féin and other so-called Republicans, but to almost every party and politician in the southern state, and to even the most moderate nationalists in the North.

It is not possible to reverse history; we cannot pretend 1916 did not happen. But we can look back from the perspective of 2011, over thirty years of death and destruction, and from a current situation in Northern Ireland which is more an armistice than a settlement, with sectarian division endemic and extremists prepared to kill in the name of Irish nationalism, and ask some questions. Have entrenched views of the history of the island since 1916 contributed to the sorry tale of the past century, and do they still constitute formidable obstacles to reconciliation in the North?

Irish nationalism today, and the Irish state, look to 1916 and the IRA campaign of 1919–21 for their household gods, their founding fathers and scriptures. From that same particular brand of nationalism come the flag, the anthem and the names of railway stations. It is a strain of nationalism characterised by two distinguishing features— reverence for the heroic use of armed force in winning independence, and independence based on total separation from Britain. Those not of that strain, such as O'Connell and Parnell, are lesser gods.

The nationalism and the state born out of 1916 both have as their greatest goal the reunification of the island; under the Belfast Agreement this is no longer demanded as of right, and Dublin is committed to recognising the legitimacy of Northern Ireland within the United Kingdom by virtue of the wishes of a majority. It is also committed, in the event of unification by agreement, to ensuring

---

3 Draft of article dated 5 April 1972, submitted to the *Sunday Press*. Original text in possession of Barbara Sweetman FitzGerald and included in this volume.

that government authority in a unified state would be exercised with 'rigorous impartiality on behalf of all the people in the diversity of their identities and traditions . . . and of parity of esteem, and of just and equal treatment for the identity, ethos, and aspirations of both communities.'[4]

With that in mind, if unification by consent did indeed come about, what sort of state would result? It could not be a state which looked back to 1916 as its great founding catharsis; it could not have the tricolour as its flag, nor 'The Soldier's Song' as its anthem, and the railway stations would need new names. The Irish language could be respected as part of the cultural heritage of many people, and as the spoken language of choice of a small minority, but could no longer be the national language, nor the first official language. Knowledge of it could not be compulsory in education or state employment.

In areas such as education and health, the new state would have to choose between ending the Catholic Church's direct involvement in ownership and control, or creating a complex apartheid system giving similar roles to all other religious groups. The Angelus would have to go. Neutrality could no longer be a keystone of foreign policy—it was and is anathema to people of a unionist background.

All this may be unthinkable to many in the South. Years ago de Valera, in one of several private conversations with Michael McInerney of *The Irish Times*, was asked if he had to choose between a united non-Gaelic Ireland, or a fully Gaelicised Irish-speaking twenty-six-county state, which would it be? After some thought Dev said it would have to be the latter.[5] His successors today may well prefer to stick with the present arrangement, leaving the Republic that eventually emerged from 1916, warts and all, more or less intact, and the troublesome North more or less sedated under the Belfast Agreement.

That would be a terrible mistake. The North has not yet totally reinvented itself, but events, and external pressures have ensured that all unionists, including hard-liners, now accept power-sharing with the minority, institutionalised cross-border cooperation, and the need to respect minority traditions and culture.

Unionists could probably live with the present arrangement,

4 See section of Belfast Agreement headed 'Constitutional Issues', 1. (v).

5 As recounted to the author by Michael McInerney, c. 1970.

but Dublin would then have to explain to the northern nationalist minority that the Belfast Agreement is not a process, but a settlement which leaves Northern Ireland within the United Kingdom, under British sovereignty, no matter how often President McAleese favours it with her official presence.[6] For Republicans, such an outcome would be close to admission of total defeat. It could work only if nationalism ceased to be the defining goal of the politics of the northern minority. In the run-up to the centenary of 1916, that is unlikely.

Conclusion

In February 2010, as the full blizzard force of the economic crisis hit southern Ireland, and job losses, bankruptcies and home repossessions multiplied, the Taoiseach, Brian Cowen, made an impassioned plea to the people for their support, for their acceptance of the painful decisions and short-term sacrifices needed to restore prosperity. And on what did he base this plea? On 1916, on its upcoming centenary, and on the need not to fail those whose sacrifice led to the foundation of the state.[7]

Patriotism, some may have thought, was as good a refuge as any for the Finance Minister/Taoiseach who had led the country into economic collapse. His speech was a reminder of the extent to which his Irishness was still defined in the context of the Easter Rising, and the narrowness that implies. It also indicated how large the centenary would loom in public discourse for the next few years.

The economic collapse, and the upheavals in the political landscape that seem to be coming in its wake, should mean there is no better time than now for a real questioning of the Ireland that has been shaped by 1916 and the hundred years since. The questioning may

6 Events and pressures from outside have forced a considerable re-thinking of Unionism—today even hard-line unionists accept cross-community power-sharing, institutionalised North-South cooperation and a say for Dublin in Northern Ireland affairs. But this re-thinking may have to go much further in light of the growing marginalisation of Northern Ireland within the United Kingdom, and the almost total omission of any consideration of Northern Ireland in recent debate at the highest political level on the future of devolution within the United Kingdom. See, for instance, the United Kingdom Government's 2007 Command Paper CM7170 *The Governance of Britain*.

7 See *The Irish Times* 5 February 2010.

have already begun; the inquests into the dead Tiger have revealed a seriously sick society in which the pursuit of wealth was the key goal, to be facilitated at every turn by the politicians. Politics itself is seen as less than healthy, and there is ever greater public disillusionment with political leaders.

The decline in church attendance, followed by the revelations of clerical abuse, make a divorce between the Catholic Church and official Irishness a possibility. Detachment of many from the Church is already the beginning of a revolution in Irish society.

But the re-inventing of Irish society and politics as envisaged in Michael Sweetman's call for a return to 1912 would mean more than a series of changes brought about by events, circumstances or political bargaining. It would require a complete re-thinking of the history of the island since 1916, by academics, politicians, the media and the people, a re-thinking that would sweep away the politics, the politicians, the money men and the demagogues who have, between them, created an economic and moral morass of Ireland.

What is needed is a revolution, not a bloody one, but a cultural and political one which could take Ireland into a post-nationalist era on this island, equipped to pursue a post-nationalist agenda in an integrating Europe.

An Irish European

Brigid Laffan*

Michael Sweetman lived to see the Irish electorate overwhelmingly endorse membership of the European Economic Community (EEC) in a referendum held on 10 May 1972. His vision for the future of Ireland was that of a country fully embedded in a supportive European framework. He wanted Ireland and the Irish to take full advantage of the opportunities offered by membership, otherwise Ireland would find itself a 'crummy suburb of England'.

Among his papers from that time is a menu from a Belgian restaurant 'Overzetboot' replete with offers of *Carbonade Flamande* and *Moules Frites au Pain,* dishes that were about to enter the culinary repertoire of a growing number of Irish people embarking on life in Brussels. Difficult as it may be to believe in the twenty-first century phase of globalisation, Brussels and the continent were foreign to the vast majority of Irish people in 1971.

Michael Sweetman did not live to see Ireland become a member of the EEC on 1 January 1973. Just five weeks after the referendum, he, together with eleven other captains of Irish industry, was killed in the Staines air disaster en route to Brussels for talks with European Commission officials on 18 June 1972. Having contributed so much to securing popular endorsement and legitimating of membership in the accession referendum, he was eager to get on with the business of preparing for membership. Was he accurate in his assessment of the impact of membership? How would Michael Sweetman assess Ireland's engagement with Europe during its thirty-eight years of membership? Would he, like his friend and Fine Gael colleague Garret FitzGerald, have continued to campaign for the EU in successive referendums?

* Brigid Laffan was Director of the Dublin European Institute based at UCD. She is the Jean Monnet Professor of European Integration within the Department of Politics at UCD and Principal of the College of Human Sciences at UCD.

The referendum campaign and the early years

As Director of the Irish Council of the European Movement, Michael Sweetman was to the forefront of the campaign that favoured membership. He campaigned tirelessly throughout the country at local meetings and university societies, wrote numerous pamphlets and newspaper articles and participated in radio and television programmes during the campaign. The accession referendum was a long campaign as befits a major decision such as membership of the EEC. Michael Sweetman was a central voice for the 'Yes' campaign. He went head to head with Micheál Ó Loinsigh of the Common Market Study Group, the leading No group, at the Mount Brandon Hotel in Tralee on 16 October 1971. Six months later, on the eve of the referendum on Tuesday 9 May, the *Evening Press* ran two articles, one in favour of membership by Michael Sweetman and one against by Micheál Ó Loinsigh. Some of the arguments made then still resonate in referendums on Europe. It is worth exploring the key arguments for membership put forward by Michael all those years ago on the eve of the referendum.

Michael Sweetman was not a dewy-eyed federalist in favour of the emergence of a European super state with powerful institutions. He was a liberal nationalist. His speeches and writings were very focused on Ireland and the EEC and on the practical benefits of membership. He saw membership of the EEC as essential to Irish prosperity and well-being. It was a project for Ireland's future captured in his statement in the *Evening Press* article: 'To seize the opportunities which membership opens up is important, not only for this generation but for our children and grandchildren too'.

On the question of full membership or associated status, he was unequivocal in his preference for full membership. In a press release (as reported in *The Irish Times* 4 November 1971), he analysed the agreements then on offer to Sweden, Switzerland and Austria and concluded that opting for trade agreements would 'mean cutting ourselves out of the advantages while still facing the problems'. He understood that a seat at the table was vital. Two of the EFTA states, Sweden and Austria, followed Ireland into the EU in the 1990s. Nor did he see membership transforming Ireland overnight. He argued that 'while EEC membership will over a period lead to many major changes in Irish life, most of these changes will be gradual' and would happen anyway but 'the effect of membership will be to speed up and intensify' modernisation. He was acutely aware of the limited capacity of small states to fashion the international system to their own liking. In November 1971, he concluded in an article in the *Irish Independent* that it was time we stopped 'theorising about how we would like the world rearranged in order to suit ourselves'. Having secured the referendum in May 1972, the challenge of membership was about to begin, a challenge that he would have relished and to which he would have contributed so much.

The practical effects of membership would, according to Michael Sweetman, involve:

1) Rapidly rising prosperity in our biggest industry, agriculture.

2) Some price increases due to higher farm prices for some products as well as rising wages.

3) Increased participation by Ireland in the decision-taking and running of the EEC.

4) A falling off in emigration and unemployment and improved job opportunities as industry expands to exploit the new market opportunities (*Irish Press*, 9 May 1972).

His assessment of the practical benefits was accurate in relation to points 1–3. In all of his writings and speeches, the opportunities for Irish agriculture and food processing in the EEC were emphasised. In addition, he understood that the government would save about £30 million annually in agricultural subsidies, money which could be used to improve welfare payments and deliver tax reliefs. Ireland began to benefit from transfers from the Common Agricultural Policy (CAP) from the outset. Not only did the Irish state transfer the subsidisation of agriculture to the EEC, but receipts from its budget for agriculture were very significant; between 1973 and 2004, 70 per cent of all budgetary largesse from Europe was from the CAP. Ireland was one of the key members of the CAP supporters' club. After accession, Irish farmers were no longer dependent on the British market where agricultural produce was sold at lower world prices. Farm incomes increased as prices for agricultural produce rose. The downside of the CAP was that consumers paid higher prices for food and the policy discriminated against third country producers, including some of the world's poorest states.

However, for Ireland it has been argued that the CAP and the growing living standards in rural Ireland facilitated the transition from a conservative society to one more comfortable with modernity. In *Black Hole, Green Card*, Fintan O'Toole suggests that EEC membership meant that the conflict between tradition and modernity in Ireland was 'resolved in favour of modernity'; the CAP bought off the 'conservative heartlands of rural Ireland'.[1] The CAP brought prosperity to the countryside, the villages and small towns and hence facilitated the development of an urban society without deep societal strain.[2]

Michael Sweetman was correct in pointing out that Ireland would increasingly participate in the running of the EEC but it is doubtful that he fully anticipated the excitement that characterised Ireland's early experiences in the Community. There was a sense of relief and exhilaration that this small state had found an external scaffolding and home in the international system. A growing number of politicians and civil servants experienced the 'red eye' flight to Brussels in the morning, participating in Council meetings, putting together the first Irish Commission *cabinet*, taking French lessons, opening up the representative offices in Brussels and entering the European Parliament. Brussels and Luxemburg were still foreign, not part and parcel of Irish governance as they are now.

It was Michael Sweetman's friend and colleague, Dr Garret FitzGerald, who provided strategic direction for Ireland's early years of membership. As Minister for Foreign Affairs he presided over the modernisation of the Department of Foreign Affairs and the preparations for Ireland's first presidency of the Council in 1975. That first presidency was superbly run by Ireland. This small state had the honour of hosting the first meeting of the European Council in Dublin Castle and completing the negotiations of the first Lomé Convention. The presidency completed Ireland's apprenticeship in the system. Dr Patrick Hillery, Ireland's first Commissioner, became a central player in developing European social policy and he took seriously the independent role of the Commission when he refused to bow to pressure from the Irish government for a delay in the introduction of the equal pay directive. In those early years, Commission officials began to ar-

1 F. O'Toole *Black Hole, Green Card* (Dublin 2003) page 19.

2 B. Laffan and J. O'Mahony *Ireland and the European Union*, (London, 2008) page 257.

rive in Ireland to assist in building up the national training agency, then called AnCO, and in-service training in companies as the Irish workforce adapted to the rigours of the larger and more demanding market. Commission officials, such as Wolfgang Stabenau and Jantina Brouwer, were very committed to Ireland and worked with the Irish government, state agencies and individual companies to modernise the skills of the Irish workforce.

When Michael Sweetman made his fourth prediction concerning the practical benefits of membership, namely that there would be a drop off in emigration and an increase in employment, he could not have foreseen the major shock to the global economic system as a consequence of the 1973 oil crisis. This was the first of two recessions in the 1970s that made Ireland's early years in the EEC very difficult. Whereas the Irish governmental system and system of public policy-making adapted with relative ease to the demands of the EEC, adaptation of the real economy was much more problematic. In a prophetic address to the IMI on 2 June 1972, just over two weeks before the fateful crash, Michael Sweetman warned Irish companies that:

> The key to survival in the new market is knowing precisely where one's opportunities lie. Those who invest the time and effort now in finding out will, if they have the equally necessary determination to act, flourish. But those who are vague about where they are going or try to go to too many different places at once, are likely to end up going nowhere at all, except out of business.

The chill winds of competition in the European market proved very challenging for Ireland in the first two decades of membership as the country learnt just what it was to be a member state. Writing after ten years of membership in 1983, Alan Matthews concluded that 'in looking at the Irish economic performance during the first decade of membership, one is struck by the evidence of lost opportunities ... Irish industry today is as structurally unsuited to providing the motor for an internationally-trading economy as it was ten years ago'. Learning to live with internationalisation proved very challenging as Ireland failed to thrive in the European economy and failed to catch up with its richer neighbours. It took until the end of the 1980s for the Irish state and social partners to begin to live with internationalisation.

Northern Ireland

Lest the discussion so far should convey the impression of a one-dimensional focus on the material benefits of Europe, a short pamphlet entitled *The Common Name of Irishman* published on 24 June 1972 just six days after his death underlines Michael Sweetman's deep concern about the deteriorating situation within Northern Ireland. The pamphlet was a discussion document that explored a number of different approaches to addressing the problems of Northern Ireland. His ideas were prescient and many of the suggestions made in the document finally came to pass in the Good Friday Agreement. He began by saying that 'The problem we face is the creation of an Ireland which every Irishman can accept' and goes on to acknowledge that the key point in any settlement 'must be the freely-given consent of both communities in Northern Ireland'. From a European perspective two things stand out in the document. First is his understanding of the impact of EEC membership on relations between Ireland and Great Britain. He said:

> Now that membership of the European Community is bringing us into a more balanced relationship with Britain, we can more easily afford to recognise the British strand in our heritage without fearing any compromise of our national integrity. We should by now have gained sufficient self-confidence to put aside its extreme attitudes of past conflicts.

I am not sure that Michael Sweetman could have imagined just how quickly membership would alter British-Irish relations. Ireland's membership of the EEC owed much to British accession. Economic dependency left us with little choice. However, within three years of membership when Britain re-negotiated the terms of membership and put it to a referendum, the Irish government of the time was adamant that if the UK were to leave the EEC, Ireland would remain a member. In just three short years, Ireland's political and psychological dependence on Britain was gone and economic dependence was being steadily eroded.

The second insight in the pamphlet related to the discussion of a Council of Ireland. Michael Sweetman intuitively understood that in the design of any constitutional settlement in Northern Ireland, 'there may be lessons to be drawn from the structure of the EEC' (page 14). The complex institutional architecture of the Good Friday Agreement and its policy remit does indeed draw on the lessons of the EEC. It begins from a model of divisible sovereignty where power can be shared across parties and states, just like the EEC. The North-South and East-West bodies fit well with Europe's emerging regionalism. The North-South Council in its sectoral composition echoes the EU Council of Ministers and the D'Hondt system for the allocation of positions within the Assembly of Northern Ireland is used in the European Parliament for the allocation of roles within the parliament to political groupings. Perhaps the most important aspect of membership, however, is the way political business is conducted in the EU. The search for consensus, the focus on engaging in low-key technical collaboration, and the respect for diversity that is fundamental to the EU, offered the communities within Northern Ireland another vision of politics.

The emergence of the Celtic Tiger

Michael Sweetman would not have been content with the manner in which Ireland failed to adjust to the economic realities of membership in the early years. He would, however, have cajoled and encouraged Ireland's political and business class to grasp the opportunities that arose following the re-launch of European integration in the mid-1980s. The Single European Act, the internal market and the doubling of EU funding to Europe's poorer regions all contributed to the emergence of the Celtic Tiger. Together with a significant increase in US investment, the stabilisation of the public finances and the emergence of a labour force with high levels of educational attainment, the conditions emerged for Ireland's golden period of economic growth. Social partnership brought industrial peace and a positive environment for investment and employment creation. The era of the dole queues ended. Ireland became the first poor member state to catch up economically with rich Europe.

The Irish boom brought the best of times to a country that had a history of relative underdevelopment, poverty, emigration and a general sense of underperformance. The speed and nature of the transition was powerfully captured by the changing image of Ireland on the covers of the *Economist*. The 1988 country report on Ireland depicted a mother and young child on her lap begging on O'Connell Bridge under the caption 'Poorest of the rich'. The association of Ireland with poverty was replaced less than ten years later with a front cover that depicted Ireland on a map of Europe as 'Europe's shining light'. The new member states that joined the EU in 2004 looked to Ireland as a model. Speaking at the new Joint Oireachtas European Affairs Committee on 6 July 2004, Brian Cowen, then Minister for Foreign Affairs, said 'many of the new member states and candidate countries see Ireland as a model, and they are particularly interested in learning from our experiences'.

Cracks were appearing, however, in Ireland's engagement with the EU and the strength of the Celtic Tiger was illusory, as we now know. In the first decade of the twenty-first century, the relationship with the EU entered a different and more challenging phase as Ireland grew in wealth and confidence. The first visible crack opened in February 2000 with the official and public reaction to the use by the Council of an early-warning system on Ireland's non-adherence to the recommendations issued to it in relation to the Broad Economic Guidelines. The Commission and Council were critical of an excessively loose fiscal policy at a time of strong inflationary pressures. The then Minister for Finance, Charlie McCreevy, was unhappy with advice from the European Commission and the reprimand from the Council at a time of budgetary surplus.

This was one of the first times when the European Commission was portrayed in Ireland as other than 'Ireland's best friend'. This was followed by a number of ministerial speeches that could be characterised as 'soft Euroscepticism'. Those speeches in summer 2000 reflected uncertainty about Ireland's place in Europe and the relative importance of the EU to Ireland. In July 2000, the Tánaiste, Mary Harney, in an address to the American Bar Association expressed her unease about the prospect of 'key economic decisions being taken at Brussels level' and the possibility that Ireland would be subject to excessive regulation. The speech is remembered largely because the Minister suggested that Ireland was nearer to Boston than Berlin, a dichotomy that entered into popular discourse. Another minister, Síle de Valera, Minister for Arts, Culture and the Gaeltacht delivered the most Euro-critical speech ever delivered by an Irish minister in Boston College, on 18 September 2000. She said that 'directives and regulations agreed in Brussels can often seriously impinge on our identity, culture and traditions'. She was not specific regarding the directives she had in mind and offered no concrete evidence to support her claims. In the speech, she called for a more vigilant, questioning attitude towards the EU and more diligence in protecting Irish interests'.

These speeches and the public spat with the Commission set the tone for the first Nice referendum in June 2001. When the ballot boxes were opened on Friday 5 June 2001, a shock awaited the Irish government, EU institutions and the candidate states. The treaty was defeated by 54 per cent to 46 per cent on a very low turnout of 34 per cent. The second Nice referendum, held on 19 October 2002, was passed by a sizeable majority of 63 per cent to 37 per cent with a turn-out of 49 per cent, significantly higher than the first. The second Nice referendum was followed by Ireland's very successful EU Presidency in the first half of 2004 that was marked by the welcome ceremony for ten new member states and the successful conclusion of the Inter-Governmental Conference on the constitutional treaty in June with Bertie Ahern chairing the European Council in June 2004.

The official narrative on Ireland's relationship with the EU was again tested in June 2008 when a majority of the Irish electorate voted against the Lisbon treaty; in a turnout of 53 per cent, 53.4 per cent voted No. This outcome was marked by a significant increase in the No vote as a proportion of the electorate, from 18 per cent to 28 per cent. An Irish government was once again faced with navigating the difficult dynamics of domestic politics and membership of the EU. The advice to the government from one of the key No voices, Sinn Féin, was clear in its submission of 18 June 2008:

> The people have now spoken and the Lisbon Treaty is over. The ratification process should now end and the leaders of the EU's 27 Member States must now negotiate a new treaty.

The government felt unable to accept this advice. Why? There were three reasons. First, the government clearly felt that Ireland's interests are best served if Ireland is, and is perceived to be, a fully engaged and committed member state. The Oireachtas Committee set up to analyse Ireland's future in the EU agreed with the government, concluding that 'Ireland's decision not to ratify the Lisbon Treaty has made the country's long-term position at the core of the European

Union considerably less certain'.[3]. Second, the government was aware that with the prospect of a UK Conservative government, Lisbon was the last opportunity for a long time to secure treaty reform in the Union. Failure to ratify the Lisbon treaty given seven years of negotiations could trigger disintegrative dynamics in Europe. That an Irish vote would give momentum to the negative European policies of the British Conservative party was at odds with Ireland's traditional positioning in the Union. Third, the government did not accept that there was a better deal on offer to Ireland. Ireland had played a major role in negotiating the treaty in the first place and would be in a much weaker position going into any future negotiations. In June 2009, the government decided to ask the Irish electorate to think again about the Lisbon treaty, having secured a set of legal guarantees on issues that were raised during the Lisbon campaign. On 2 October 2009, the Irish electorate returned a very different verdict. With a turnout of 59 per cent, 67.1 per cent of voters voted Yes and 32.9 per cent voted No.

There is no doubt that Michael Sweetman would have been at the hustings during the many referendums on European treaties since 1972 and particularly following the two No votes. He would have been part of the civil society mobilisation that contributed so much to the turnaround.

Just how Europeanised is Ireland?

Notwithstanding the benefits of over thirty years of membership, Michael Sweetman might well have concluded that Ireland is weakly Europeanised. The Irish political class does not have strong ties in Europe, Irish electoral politics rewards those who are locally active and engaged. Activity such as scrutiny of European directives in parliamentary committees, or engagement in European affairs is not rewarded. Deep knowledge of the EU is limited to those who have had ministerial experience in the key ministries that deal with Brussels, opposition spokespeople, parliamentary committee members and MEPs. Party to party relations in the European Parliament, particularly for Fianna Fáil, have been marginal thus far. This may change with membership of the Liberal grouping following the 2009 European elections.

3 Oireachtas Report, November 2008, page 3.

Irish voters combine a diffuse support for EU membership with a low level of knowledge of how the EU works. In Eurobarometer polls, the Irish are among those who regard membership of the EU as a good thing and a significant majority maintain that Ireland has benefited from EU membership. In 2007, 86 per cent of those surveyed felt that Ireland has benefited from EU membership, the highest proportion in the EU (compared with an EU average of 59 per cent). Seven per cent of Irish people believed that Ireland has not benefited from being a member of the EU, in contrast with 36 per cent of Germans, 44 per cent of British and 46 per cent of Cypriots.

The Irish, however, do not know the EU very well. In a 1995 study of levels of knowledge of the EU, Richard Sinnott discovered that the positive perceptions of EU membership in Ireland were accompanied by relatively low levels of knowledge regarding the EU. The Milward Brown study conducted in 2008 after the Lisbon referendum concluded that:

> It is clear from these findings that the 'lack of information/knowledge' problem that underpins the No vote, goes well beyond the boundaries of the Lisbon Treaty. The knowledge deficit extends into basic understanding of the EU itself and this is particularly the case for those who voted No to the Lisbon Treaty.

The report went on to say that there was 'very limited awareness, even among those educated to a high level, of how the EU operates'.

A majority of Irish people have not added a European identity to their national identity. Across Europe, a majority are comfortable describing themselves as both their nationality and European whereas the data for Ireland shows the 'nationality only' identity trumps 'nationality and European'. The layered identity proclaimed grandiosely by Stephen Daedalus in *A Portrait of the Artist* when he gave himself the following address *County Kildare, Ireland, Europe, The World, The Universe* was not for the majority of Irish people. The narrative on Ireland and Europe, with its focus on benefits, particularly financial transfers, has left the Irish bereft of a broader cultural frame within which to position Ireland in Europe. Certainly, growing affluence and increased travel have brought European foods and tastes into Irish homes and restaurants. Throughout Ireland there are continental-style cafés that vie with the traditional communal outlet, the pub. And all major European cities have their Irish pub. Although 75 per cent of second level students take a continental language for the Leaving Certificate, proficiency in actually speaking continental languages is very varied. At third level, language departments have come under considerable pressure with a decline in the number of students taking languages at universities. Latin, for long the *lingua franca* of the Catholic Church in Ireland and elsewhere, provided a strong link to a very ancient Europe. In 'Alphabets' Seamus Heaney recalls how, studying Latin: *'Declensions sang on air like a hosanna'* as the class explored the columns of the elementary textbook.

Greek and Latin, so much part of the Irish second level curriculum in the past, have now virtually disappeared. In 2008 a total of 116 students took higher level Latin at Leaving Certificate level. The classical curriculum was a direct link to that intensive engagement between Ireland and Europe that marked the first millennium. On 11 June 2008, Pope Benedict XVI spoke of the Irish monk Columbanus as 'one of the fathers of Europe'. He went even further in reminding his audience that Columbanus, in 600 AD, was the very first person to use the phrase *'totius Europae'* (all of Europe).[4] The Irish Colleges in Louvain, Salamanca, Paris, Lisbon and Rome were not just religious centres but centres of diplomacy from the sixteenth century onwards. An undue focus on the material aspect of EU membership since 1973 has left many Irish people without a sense of our European past.

Reflections

Michael Sweetman did not live to see Ireland's engagement with Europe over the last forty years. He missed the early excitement as the world of Brussels opened up to Irish society and he did not witness the growing pains experienced by Ireland in the EU, particularly in the economic realm. Michael Sweetman would have constantly reminded the Irish that membership of the EU was an opportunity but one that had to be grasped. Even before membership, he was warning Irish firms that they would have to adapt to the demands of an open economy and would have to remain competitive if they were to seize the opportunities. He would have gloried in Ireland's catch-up with the core economies in the 1990s and, given his concern about compet-

4 I am indebted to my UCD colleague Dr Pádraic Conway for bringing this quote to my attention.

itiveness, would have acted as a voice of caution during the worst exuberance of the Celtic Tiger years. The fracture in Ireland's European policy that appeared in 2000 and the outcome of the two referendums on Nice and Lisbon would have troubled him. There is no doubt that he would have joined Garret FitzGerald on the hustings and would have advised the Irish people to hold on to the moorings provided by the EU to this small state. He would have found it inconceivable that Ireland could have thrown away economic prosperity through reckless domestic policies and a weakness of regulation. It would have been unimaginable to him that a rich Ireland would have needed a bailout from the EU and IMF. His Ireland, with per capita incomes about 55 per cent the average of EEC incomes at the time, did not have a reputation for fiscal irresponsibility.

That said, faced with the present upheaval, Michael Sweetman would have turned his attention to the future, to how this small state could renew and rebuild its economy and polity. We owe it to the builders and modernisers of the Irish state, economy and society to find that future.

Images of Michael, my father

Rachel Sweetman

I realise as I start this that I have only happy memories of my father, which says a lot in itself.

Apart from the sadness of losing him when I was nine, but, even then, I had the feeling the loss would deepen and stretch me.

It's the images of him that I love.

I see him in his big, baggy, black woolly britches, big woolly jumper covered in fuzzballs from the fruitfarm in Meath, hair tousled. I see him driving the car on the way there, with us in the trailer along with the bags of soot we collected from the chimney sweep for the raspberry canes. I hear the house filled with the music of Mozart and Bach on Sunday mornings, a resounding 'all is well'.

I see him eating his muesli when it was new here and we didn't know what it was.

He was playful, relaxed, warm, earthy, hardworking and loving. He seemed to live life to the full with lots of interests and hobbies, and family was always most important. With all of us gathered around him he planted eight apple trees in the garden in Dublin in a long row, one for each member of the family going down in age and blessed with the nicknames he gave us. I was 'mophead'. (Still am!).

I remember him putting us barefoot into big wooden barrels to trample the apples for the cider he was making. We used to pick elderflowers along the road for wine.

He used to tickle me from head to toe 'til I could hardly breathe!

I loved that he would read the *Beano*.

I only grieved for him nineteen years after he died when I started training as a psychotherapist. The grief came up unexpectedly over two winters, whenever I had some quiet time. Grieving cured my asthma and drew me much closer to him again. I still feel him close and available, and it feels good to still miss him at times as an adult, and to shed the odd tear.

Brendan Halligan*

Interviewed by Caroline Stephenson

When do you remember first meeting Michael?

To be perfectly honest, I cannot remember when I first met him, but there was a sort of circle—I suppose you could put it like that—in Dublin at the time. Mary Robinson was there, to my memory, and Denis Corboy of course was the spider in the web bringing everyone together. And there was an interesting relationship between the people in the Labour Party in that circle and the people in Fine Gael. There was a strong sort of social democratic element in Fine Gael, Declan Costello and Michael and so on; Garret FitzGerald and then . . . people like Conor Cruise O'Brien and Justin Keating and Michael O'Leary. And whereas political commentators at the time might have been looking at the parties being in conflict or opposition with each other and any future arrangement being impossible, there was a very strong relationship on a personal level—mainly because of the ideology, for the want of a better word . . . We would have, therefore, shared a sort of reformist, strong reformist agenda.

Now the Labour Party were social democrats, but at the human level of the relationship that we all have with each other, I thought it was a very important component of Irish political life at the time. I mean, I had just become general secretary of the Labour Party in or around that time and, contrary to a lot of subsequent re-writing of history, I found it a very interesting, exciting time and very vibrant. And I suppose, in one sense, what also bound us all together and gave another dimension to the relationship was a genuine interest in and love for the European idea.

Right, even though Labour at the time were publicly opposed to joining.

Yes, but in the group that I just mentioned every one of those peo-

* Brendan Halligan was an MEP from 1983 to 1984. Chairman of the Institute of International Affairs. He has been a member of the Irish Council of the European Movement. He is currently the Policy Coordinator for the Labour Party.

ple would have been very strongly pro-European. So we had a problem, because the party as a whole was opposed to Irish membership. But I had joined the Irish Council for the European Movement—as it was called at the time—at the invitation, of course, of Denis Corboy, who was inviting everybody and pulling all the strings. You actually knew it was happening, but you didn't mind; he was a charming man; he remained a friend all my life . . . And the relationship amongst that group of people—sort of ten people, I suppose—was very strong, and it brought the two parties together into government in '73. Denis was behind the scenes, of course, and he was then heading up the EEC office and I can remember one lunch in particular in his office which he orchestrated—amongst [them were] the people that I mentioned; numbers of them now by this point were Ministers in the government—and he wanted something to happen or recommended that something should be happening. And it did, and it was very important. So the European thing at this stage would have been very, very, very powerful and we had this problem of explaining it to our colleagues in Fine Gael. They understood that we had to get through the referendum . . . So it was very much sort of a strong, reformist agenda . . . Michael would have, I think, slotted in to both camps. That would have been the interesting thing about him. Garret worked with him as well, but I knew him from the reform agenda and the European agenda.

And would you have had many dealings with Michael during that time?

Mainly through the European Movement, and, to a certain extent, because he was writing; to a certain extent through the reform agenda. I would have known him, but the relationship I suppose never had the chance of maturing to the point of a long one, you know? But I was very interested in his ideas.

And Michael, do you think he would have had a political future?

I do. It was a great tragedy because first of all he had already established himself as a serious thinker and mover and shaker on the Fine Gael side, and he had this good relationship with the Labour Party. We got the opportunity then to do something about it later, and he would have been part of it and he would have contributed, I think, as well in areas other than the ones I have already mentioned.

I think he would have been very good on industrial [matters]. So it is one of those occasions you can say someone was lost almost before their career began. He showed a great deal of promise and potential, and the only way you know promise and potential can be literally translated into practice is by living and availing of the possibilities ... The general reaction was that this was a terrible tragedy ... a great loss to society. I mean, this is a difficult thing to say to his widow or his children, you know, as if they were worried about that.

Yes, there was a palpable sense of loss of a great talent, and it's interesting then that it came back in a number of ways: you know, in lectures and that sort of stuff, and the fact that you are thinking of doing this book. It is an indication of the fact that he is well remembered. There are not too many people about whom you can get a book even suggested and that people would be willing to write after such a long passage of time ... We will be remembering things past on the one hand, and reflecting on an opportunity of a talent that never was given the chance to flower.

Would Fine Gael have been a different party had he lived? That is a very theoretical question.

It's a very reasonable question to ask. He certainly would have been a minister; he certainly would have been a figure of considerable weight in the government. And as to what would have happened after Liam Cosgrave's departure is anyone's guess, but he was certainly of leadership quality. Fine Gael was lucky in the sense that it had two people at least at the time, you know—Garret and Declan. Declan decided for his own personal reasons not to continue in politics and left in 1976, and had Michael been around, what can I say? He would certainly have been in the frame.

When you say talent and loss to society, could you maybe elaborate on that?

Well, the key requirement in politics is to have the ability to think about the future; to imagine, as distinct from managing the here and now—a lot of people can do that, and most of them that can do it should be civil servants. The evolution of policy and also national strategy which was different then, there are not too many people that can do that, so I think this is where he was missed. Take, for example, the European thing. To have understood very early on that Ireland's destiny lay with this organisation and association of the nations ... He had a capacity to understand that the destiny lay inside an emerging European Union; [this] was very significant because the country was, I wouldn't say parochial, but coming bloody close to saying it, and to have the capacity to think outside the island and to understand what was happening elsewhere and that we should be a part of it, that was given to a very few people.

Those who were pushing the European agenda would have been tolerated regardless; I suppose also those who had begun to address the social agenda would have been regarded as a bit eccentric, especially in Fine Gael. You know, the ethos in Fine Gael was either very sound commercial men, or the lawyers, or the big farmers, and they didn't necessarily pre-occupy themselves too much with the rest of the population, you know. So to bring that particular type of perspective into play was quite unusual ... it was the presence of that element in Fine Gael that made a coalition possible. I mean, I consciously pushed this idea at the time and I had therefore no difficulty coming from where we were supposed to be coming, from the left and that sort of stuff in saying that we should be in government with Fine Gael because, 'look there is an element that I would be delighted to have in the Labour Party and with whom we could work because we have a common agenda in terms of social reform'. Michael was part of that. So I think when you begin to measure up what would have happened and what might he have contributed had he lived, what might you say? He could have been a Minister for Justice; he had a very strong reform programme. I now understand the forces we were up against; I didn't understand exactly then the extent of it and how deep their tentacles lay in sections.

But I think he would have been very helpful. He could equally have contributed to a very strong industrial policy. So there were a number of areas in which he could have played a role. And the thing about politics is that suddenly you are thrown into an area you don't necessarily have an expertise in, but a good political figure, a good public figure, is somebody who can just suddenly start doing it. So, for example, he would have been a very good Foreign Minister.

And at the time, what sort of qualities would you have recognised?

A particular type of, you could say, gentleman of the old school sort of thing . . . Fine Gael produced such people. Such people didn't exist in the Labour Party, you know what I mean people like Garret FitzGerald and Declan Costello particularly, and Tom O'Higgins whose name I haven't mentioned; he was a fantastic guy. Jim Dooge was also part of this group. They were quite a remarkable group and he was part of that group. Lovely disposition, very nice guy, very good. Good moral compass and an intellect to go with it. I also thought there was an element of steeliness about him. He might have been tougher in pursuing his ambitions for Irish society, let me put it like that, than perhaps some of his Fine Gael contemporaries. I am not going to mention any one name, but Fine Gael people sometimes were too nice, especially fighting Fianna Fáil.

Can I just point out that the Labour Party itself was going through a profound transition and it had all the traditional elements of a Labour Party? It was a very strong rural party which was difficult to come to terms with. It mainly was composed of rural workers and their representatives; mainly trade union officials, not necessarily known for their intellectual gifts. And then there was a newer Labour Party, which was basically Dublin but there were elements elsewhere.

Intelligentsia?

Intelligentsia type of thing. So these two parties didn't necessarily reside happily side by side all the time, but that new Labour Party was being led by a man who was from the country and who had a big, strong trade union background; he wanted to transform the politics of the country, but wanted to transform his own party first. It was that element of the Labour Party that was linking up with the new element of Fine Gael. So you have these two more traditional elements that would have found it very difficult to work with and there was this bridge being created between these two to the point where—I don't know whether this has been written down; I have no problem writing about it or talking about it—we had regular meetings that were dealing with our common interests, not least preparing the way to government. They would have mainly been held in Declan Costello's house. Nobody in the media ever picked up on the fact that we were all meeting. Jim Dooge would have been at these, and Garret, of course, and Alexis FitzGerald.

Michael O'Leary?

Michael O'Leary and also Justin Keating and myself. By the way, those meetings were the bridge; that was the point on which the two parties locked together and it was the personal relationships at that point [which] were indispensible for later creating a huge foundation. I ended up writing a Programme for Government in 1973 with Jim and then in 1977 I ended up writing it with Alexis. So we just completely trusted the other and we were never suspicious of the other. Denis Corboy was great.

What did Denis do? I remember meeting him shortly before the plane crash. How was he involved?

Denis was a barrister who recognised the significance of the EEC. He saw that we weren't in any way involved, even at the official level; no-one was thinking about it. So he made contact with Monnet, the first President of the Commission and as a result Denis set up an office in Dublin for the Action Committee for Europe which Monnet had founded. This was around 1967. Denis operated as an unofficial ambassador/organiser, he has this gift of networking with people and he brought many people of disparate views together.

You were saying Michael was a gentlemanly type of person. What did you mean by that?

I mean the best type; just very mannerly, very considerate and very kind. There was a genuineness about him, a cultured man. Very good personal relations; someone you can trot out without any fears and a great mind, a European mind, which is very important.

Jim Dooge*

Interviewed by Caroline Stephenson

Jim Dooge began with recalling how he had come to know Michael Sweet-man.

In the early years of the European Movement, I was in Cork. I only came [back] up [to Dublin] in 1970, so we were quite close both in Fine Gael and the European Movement from 1970 to 1972.

Just those two years; had you encountered him before that?

I couldn't tell you, really. I was in the Senate all right and we probably would have had some contact, but as I say I don't remember much detail; I just remember liking him.

You might have known about his political ideas?

Well they were close to my own in those days . . . I had been in the Senate since '61, and from '61 to '65 James Dillon was the leader. One day at the meeting of the parliamentary party, Tony Esmonde from Wexford—whose father had been an MP but he was really of the Redmondite tradition—said that we shouldn't follow a certain thing because Fine Gael was not a radical party. I remember James Dillon, to my surprise, saying 'Fine Gael is a radical policy and the day it ceases to be a radical party I will cease to be a member'.

I went into politics in 1948. I came home one evening—I was working at the ESB at the time—and my wife told me she had rung Fine Gael in the morning. And in the middle of the afternoon Liam Cosgrave rang to see what relation I was to John P. Dooge; so typical of Liam's closeness to his constituents. So I joined in October/November '47 and there was an election in February '48; I spoke on the back of a lorry in Dalkey. After the election—at that time Dublin County was one constituency with five seats—the new split came in,

* Jim Dooge (1922–2010) was simultaneously a world figure in the study of hydrology and climate change, and an important contributor to Irish political life, serving as a Fine Gael Senator from 1961 to 1977 and 1981 to 1987. He served briefly as Minister for Foreign Affairs, and made important contributions to the EU, serving as Chairman of the Committee which led to the Single European Act and the Maastricht Treaty.

with two three-seat constituencies. Liam asked me to become secretary of the new constituency executive. This happened in March and it gives you the picture of politics in the lead up to the new departures. Liam said to me one time, 'I want you to go down to Blackrock and I want you to take over Blackrock branch'. He said there was some fiddling of petrol coupons during the election and he wanted rid of the chairman. I said, 'but I don't know anyone in Blackrock', and he said, 'you go down to 40 Sweetman's Avenue and ask for Jim Gill.' Jim worked as a bin man in Dún Laoghaire. He was virtually illiterate; he was one of the best political brains I ever knew. A week later I walked in to my first meeting in Blackrock branch and walked out chairman; it's amazing the way these things happen.

As I say, I had been very close to Liam Cosgrave and we got on very well. In fact in 1965, I was on the Fine Gael front bench in the Senate and actually was Cathaoirleach. So then up till 1970 I was still living in Cork and you asked me when did I first meet Michael? I just don't know. The thing is that I wasn't then in on the business of Declan Costello and the Just Society. I agreed with it, but I wasn't in on the formation of it. Also at that time, I wasn't on the parliamentary party front bench, so I didn't know about the committee that Liam chaired. Liam chaired the committee that looked at the thing and recommended it. I would have known after coming to Dublin in 1970 that Michael was active in this particular area, but I wouldn't have known the extent of it. So the thing is that I have this memory of him as particularly from the point of view of European affairs, but also from the Fine Gael point of view.

And what was your impression of his contribution to politics at the time?

I thought it was immense. I thought his loss was very, very great indeed. I think he would have had a real future in politics. I think he would have had a real role; he wouldn't have had to wait until Garret came along. Liam took power in 1973. I always had and still have great friendship with Liam. People think of him as being ultra-conservative, but he wasn't. He was a quiet man; a good chairman. Michael listened to people, so I think that he would have found a role either in the party, or perhaps even in the Senate at that time. Declan sort of withdrew—I remember myself and Paddy Harte going up to Declan trying to persuade him to stay, but not to any avail—so I think he would have had a real role to play under Liam, because Liam was very good at making use of people with ideas.

Would you have worked quite closely with Michael?

Not for long, you see? My memory is of being quite close with him, but then I was involved with European Affairs for so long that I forget what the issues were in that short two-year period.

And what would your memories be of him at that time?

I would say a quite gentle person, who was very enthusiastic and very efficient. That's the best summary I can give. He made a very real contribution to the European Movement, as I say, and it's only a pity that our connection wasn't longer.

And then you weren't really involved with the Just Society?

No, but I'll tell you a story of a later policy. At a later period, there had been a lot of discussion between Alexis, Garret and myself about the necessity for developing policy. One time it was decided to try to set up a policy committee in Fine Gael and the two of them suggested I write to Liam, as I had the best relationship with Liam. So I wrote to him suggesting the party set up a policy committee to look at future policy. I wanted it to be a full party committee, not just an ad hoc committee. It was very interesting the reply I got from Liam. I got a letter back saying, 'Dear Jim, if you think this is a good idea, go ahead with it'. He wouldn't commit to it himself. So that was the sort of Liam attitude; he would accommodate ... But the thing is that from 1965 on Gerry Sweetman influenced Liam against Garret. Garret had come into the Senate in 1965; Liam was very much influenced by Garret in the first year. Then when Garret went off to France in the summer, Gerry Sweetman started turning Liam against him and I remember also John Healy—who was Backbencher [*The Irish Times* columnist] —was stirring up trouble by referring to dissidents within Fine Gael.

That would have been Garret?

Garret, Alexis and myself. I was in Cork one time sitting in my office and the phone rang and it was Gerry Sweetman. He said 'Backbencher in *The Irish Times* this morning mentioned that you were one of the people conspiring; you have to issue a denial. I said, 'issuing for something like that is confirmation, I have done nothing of the sort'. Actually it was about the time that we were trying to get this policy committee going. We would sometimes meet for lunch, and I think this was interpreted as a conspiracy.

And would this have been why Gerry was against?

He was very right wing. He was a very able Minister for Finance. The interesting thing about Gerry Sweetman was that he was very right wing in his policy, but he was the man that promoted Whitaker over the heads of others. He gave Whitaker his big jump in the Department of Finance. Yes, that's why I mentioned it to you; it's an interesting thing.

I'll tell you another story. There was a Fine Gael Ard Fheis and two young members brought forward a motion. One was Vincent Browne and the other was Henry Kelly. [The motion] was that the name of the Fine Gael party be changed from Fine Gael: United Ireland to Fine Gael: the Social Democratic Party. This was debated; some people objected from the floor. I was on the front bench at the time and I spoke from the stage; I intervened. They said this could never be done, and I said 'I don't see why it can't be done, after all we believe in social reform through democratic action. Why can we not be social democrats?' It was passed by the Ard Fheis, but Gerry Sweetman pointed out that a change of the name was a change in the constitution and that it would have to be approved of by the branches in the country. He organised its rejection.

Donal Flynn*

Interviewed by Caroline Stephenson

The interview commenced with Donal Flynn reflecting on an earlier conversation.

You said because of Michael's talent in politics and other talents, social talents and his work and his frame of mind, which was very effective in the Confederation of Irish Industry, you said he was the sort of person who could be Taoiseach, and I sort of politely said 'hmm haw yes I suppose', but very, very improbable for a range of reasons. First of all, we were all enormously [involved], including himself. He was pretty central, but still only central to a fairly peripheral group of society. Now it was true to say that Garret FitzGerald reached power and there would have been a certain resonance between Garret and Michael in their general philosophy, but it would be an illusion to think that the coincidence of mentality, which I would not exaggerate, would have meant that Michael would be preferred to be a Minister of something. With a coalition government FitzGerald would have just ten ministries to give out, or something, and he would be taking geographic things into account and party turf bosses to be satisfied, and you are immediately going to see that an individual's talent does not carry them that far. The second thing is that the particular talent needed to be Taoiseach or even a Minister but particularly Taoiseach, the most obvious is one of assembling all the necessary votes, not only in your party but in the Dáil, so it's a ward heeler. The classic person who becomes Taoiseach is Bertie; so it's interesting pub talk or it's an interesting thing to mull over. But actually neither the circumstances nor the particular talents or characteristics of that man will have said 'oh he will be Taoiseach'

---

* Donal Flynn was chairman of the Fine Gael Central Branch when Michael Sweetman was on the committee. He was part of a ginger group which produced the pamphlet *The Will to Win* which won them the title 'Young Tigers' from James Dillon. He ended his involvement with politics after Michael's death.

And what about Michael then? You would not have seen a role for him in politics?

What it really means is that you cannot extrapolate, except in the most fanciful way, from where he was then to what he might have become; that is a very rocky road and a very twisty road and a very unreliable road. You wouldn't know . . . His strengths wouldn't neces- sary have still remained effective in office. You just go in nine to five or nine to six or nine to nine or six in the morning till twelve at night, and do some particular job you are given with a very low probability of getting a job that particularly suited you or that particularly fitted your mentality or philosophy or something. People are just slotted in to fill spaces rather than fill roles, so it is fanciful to talk or to imagine where it would all have gone.

Yes, so may be we should just start then with when you first met Mi- chael?

The first meeting was when we were both on the Committee of the Central Branch of Fine Gael, which was two things. It purported to be something of a policy forming branch in the sense that they were people of a bookish kind or educated or trying to use ideas; they were middle-class people in politics who weren't going for office, who were part of policy formation in their own minds. They were interested in ideas and that committee was not directly connected with the making of policy because there wasn't any making of policy. Gerry Sweetman and Liam Cosgrave abhorred any crystallisation of ideas; they found them a big nuisance. Liam Cosgrave, in my conversations with him when I was speech writing for him, made it quite clear that, not in any hostile way, but made it clear in his behaviour and his analysis that the handshaking in the constituencies got the seats and fancy statements which might upset one or other person were very unlikely to bring you a majority. So that's the policy formation or the policy interest of those people and it was very flaky, and in no sense focused, even there on that committee. But I would say that it became an organisational thing because I was good at that.

But to go back to policy: what therefore happened was that policy formation began to develop outside of the party with the principal known names, Declan Costello and Garret FitzGerald, and that was the beginning for Michael; Michael then moved up and had standing in that circle. But Michael was not a theoretician or certainly not an ideologue; the characteristic of his thinking was pragmatism. You know, there are so many poor people; you need jobs; you need efficiency and so forth. So this assumption of the validity of just thinking and acting directly would be his characteristic rather than any grandiose plan. I remember him talking about the negative reaction within the Confederation of Irish Industry. So many voices: you know we'll never do that; we wouldn't know how to do that; you know in Ireland, we wouldn't be able to do that. Michael had this gesture of flinging his arms out at the shoulder and saying 'WHY NOT, WHY NOT? Of course we can do it!' We learnt to do it. So that was focused in turn in getting into the EU. The British Irish Free Trade Area had started to work, this would be now 1964 that sort of time.

It was that early, this was the first time you would have met then?

1964, 1965, quite early, yes. You had the first tax concessions for export tax relief, for example. The context in which these efforts were being made to look out and behave as adults in the larger trading world was extraordinarily dull and dire, poor and impoverished. People were poor; the population was 2.9 million; people were flooding out all the time. There was a strong sense of combined desperation and pioneering to just say this show just won't do at all. And, as Ken Whitaker has illustrated a few times, the first of all struggle in the administration was to leave off the old self sufficiency rule of the 1930s and the 1940s very much associated with Fianna Fáil and the small farmers, and secondly to recognise that the creation of wealth was legitimate and necessary. There is a book that sums up this period very accurately and reflects the lectures I had been getting in UCD from Jimmy Meenan and Paddy Lynch. Tom Garvin, the Professor of Politics in UCD, has written a book *Preventing the Future: Why was Ireland so poor for so long?* and that book will tell you the tone of the times and what we were reacting against and leaving behind so in that context. It will actually describe it, the whole thing. Irish priests making sermons about the virtues of poverty combined with the horrors of pagan England; 27 per cent of the schools were 'A' schools, primary schools teaching entirely through Irish so when I left the Christian Brothers in Nenagh the boys there, many of them literally in rags, had received only an Irish medium education, stopped school at fourteen waited until after they were sixteen and then emigrated as hewers of wood and drawers of water.

This is the early sixties?

Yes. Well, that regime in the schools went on until 1973 when Dick Burke eliminated the condition that you couldn't get any Leaving Cert piece of paper at all unless you passed in Irish and since there was only the Catholic University with its condition of getting in with Irish, you couldn't get into University unless you went to Trinity and if you were a believing Catholic you couldn't go to Trinity without a letter from John Charles McQuaid so the draconian nature of the controls of the society would be hard to recapture. But secondly, our psychological indifference was already old hat, but the structures were there and if you take something like Irish, the structures are still there; you can't get into UCD without Irish today, so the distortion of a country trying to make something of itself with the constraints, were very heavy. But Michael would be up with the leading edge with the Confederation of Irish Industry, but again he wouldn't be much into denouncing the prevailing philosophy or commenting on it in, let's say, anti-clerical terms or class warfare terms or anything like that. He would be just pragmatic. He'd just say of course it should be done; it'd be ridiculous not to do it.

He would look at the problem and try to see a solution.

Yes. I think politics would have probably dragged him down because it does grind you very hard. Being a backbencher, they are reasonably well paid now, but back then they were very badly paid. I would place him more easily amongst the real leaders of Irish industry. So that combination of pragmatism and intelligence and sense of scope I would place, now if I had to imagine him, twenty or thirty years later, it would be as a leader in that segment rather than a political one . . .

What did appear to me to be relevant was that as Michael and Barbara got interested in the North in the terrible times with the terrible killings, that I wouldn't be surprised if that became really the more serious and contact work, and more serious constructive, committed work and more obviously overwhelming and demanding because you can't go on very long in a Fine Gael opposition party working on ideas. You are not in power; the party itself doesn't gain this power and when it does, it doesn't gain it through ideas. It is just from electoral dynamics: people just get fed up with Fianna Fáil and vote for Fine Gael. You don't want ideas because of risks of alienating some of the people who might drift over and so you wouldn't expect anybody to go on two, four, six, eight years just typing up ideas for Fine Gael. They would be saying, 'how long can I do this?'

There's a shelf life!

Exactly. So it was therefore all that that circle passed on, but also when the Just Society was being pushed in to FG, the old timers or most people resisted it. The party as a whole didn't embrace it. Again not for any bad reason, it wasn't a way to power and if you felt those things, there was already anyway the modernistic trend towards better health service, or social welfare. The economic change would hold up the problems of having the resources for those, so it didn't necessarily need an ideal or a philosophic formulation. The philosophic formulation was then in turn weak and in technical terms of very mixed quality. Also there was never an ideological resistance in the governing institutions to better social welfare or something like that; it was only a matter of money, so persuasion wasn't needed. What was needed was better technique, to get the money, to get wealthier, and to proceed into a modern society, but it didn't actually need crusading. It wasn't like the Labour Party in 1912 in England or something, all that period of leftwing struggle wasn't needed.

Why?

Because it was already current: France, Germany, England . . . and there was a sense of community and nationhood and assumption that people needed to be looked after. And it was lectured already widely in universities. So you didn't have to jump on a soap box to persuade people to vote, you just had to go on and do it, but to go on and do it you had to be in Government.

Right, so it wasn't that radical at the time?

Not in concept, to push it and make it happen was a political task. The committee I was on—which was in social welfare—there were 23 meetings, chaired by Paddy Belton. There was no way of bringing cohesion to the Social Welfare Committee. Garret just forgot about it and went and got his own typewriter and locked himself in the lavatory and wrote up his own thing or whoever did it, I don't know. But for example, the little bit I did there was to insert or have adopted that payments should be made to unmarried mothers. I don't know what we are to call them now—single parents? —but unmarried mothers didn't get money and of course it was against that context that so many of them ended up in those strange places like the Magdalene and so forth.

. . .

The idea of socialism, it wouldn't again be a doctrinaire, but it would be people understanding their interests which we saw again much later in the first divorce referendum, which Garret tried to push through. Before that it would have given freedom to the Oireachtas to legislate for divorce, and people were asked to vote not knowing what law the Oireachtas would pass. And it only got through the second time when the referendum contained the constraints on what the Oireachtas could pass. The first time out there wasn't even a law that guaranteed a farming widow that she would get the farm! So people quite correctly could see this as—Alice Glenn said, this is 'turkeys voting for Christmas'. You are just going to pass some law that this nutcase up in Dublin is thinking about and next thing you won't have any rights to the farm. So they had to pass statute laws to guarantee the inheritance or the portion of the farming wife. The Catholics did manage to get in and you know weaken some aspects of the thing, making it a bit more awkward to help people with divorces. But that would be a property issue rather than anything the government could focus on.

Most of it boils down to money anyway, doesn't it, particularly with the Church?

Yes, that was one of my debates with Michael. In those days the debates were whether there should be divorce or whether there should be contraception allowed. So we both agreed completely that it was none of the State's business to be interfering with contraception and the Church was getting out of its sphere that they should all shag off or some other technical term. But I just said to Michael that divorce was State business; that the organisation of those relationships and property and all the rest was State business and the State just couldn't say anybody that gets divorced would have a complete free load. That was social management, it was State business. So we used to disagree about that at that stage.

Most of what we were talking about at the time was done, after-wards. The reason we were talking about it was because it was natu-rally wanted. But I wasn't surprised even at the time when Michael and Barbara entered into the circle of people directly engaged in the Northern business. Again I was off and married at the time; I was only strongly in contact with Michael for two or three years and maybe a fraction longer, but for a short period. It was quite clear that this was just much more serious than anything else. The problem was much more worth his salt, his skills and the high level of idealism and the concept of centralisation and the social skills to build those bridges and to be able to do that.

Culture and religion in Ireland, 1960–2010

Enda McDonagh*

The years of Michael Sweetman's historical life were few, much too few, but the period, 1935–72, was, globally, as dramatic, destructive and transformative as any in history. Ireland was on the margin of much of this. Its geography, combined with its recent and traumatic birth as a self-governing state, left it at arm's and armies' length from the powerful dramas unfolding about it. Of course, it was not entirely untouched by the military, political and economic struggles in the larger world. Indeed, the impact of these struggles, combined with the aftermath of its own struggles in the earlier part of the century, made the 1930s, the 1940s and the 1950s grim enough decades. The stagnant economy, with mass unemployment, accelerating emigration and widespread poverty addressed by only minimal health and social services, made it the very poor relation of Europe. And for many critics there was religious and cultural stagnation also.

I only met Michael Sweetman once, at the home of Joan and Garret FitzGerald. I was, however, closely involved with some of the movements, ideas and ideals which shaped the causes to which he was dedicated. I had been an early and active member of Tuairim in the 1950s and into the 1960s—a quite significant intellectual and social think-tank which introduced a new level of debate to the Irish political and economic issues; including fisheries and agriculture, North-South relations and numerous other political and cultural problems. Through the *National Observer* I came to know Alexis FitzGerald and then Declan Costello and their Just Society project. All of these en-

---

* Enda McDonagh was Professor of Moral Theology and Canon Law at the Pontifical University at Maynooth from 1958 to 1995. In the early sixties he founded the InterChurch Association of Moral Theology. He was appointed an Ecumenical Canon at St Patrick's Cathedral in 2007.

gaged Michael Sweetman on his return to Ireland.

These were the decades of my youth and of Michael Sweetman's. They are introduced here as prologue to the more adventurous and dynamic decades to follow.

Religion and culture

In some discourses, particularly those prevalent among churchmen in the first half of the 20th century, culture, taken in its broadest sense as the whole way of life of a people, is presumed to include religious beliefs and practices as part of that way of life. In other discourses religion and culture are at least semi-distinguished and semi-detached. I will be favouring the latter course here, although conscious of how confusing, inadequate and in need of correction such a course may sometimes be.

The distinction and the tension between sacred and secular became explicit in the West with the Enlightenment of the 18th century and its philosophical, scientific, cultural and political offspring. Similar forces were already at play and in struggle for thousands of years but the various dimensions were not so distinctively denominated and set in opposition. Perhaps oddly in the current Irish context, Christianity, with its doctrine of a transcendent God and the consequent demolition of the pagan gods, has even been regarded as the source of secularization. Giving to Caesar what was Caesar's and to God what was God's has been interpreted as the template for secular politics.

As one conventional view has it, the 1930s, 1940s and 1950s of the 20th century were in Ireland as stagnant religiously and culturally as they were politically, economically and socially. Recent careful and sympathetic readings, by Louise Fuller for religion and Brian Fallon for culture, reveal a more nuanced picture. The once legally prohibited Catholic faith and an oppressed Catholic people had reached, as it was believed, full freedom with the establishment of the independent Irish state. Serious limitations remained. In Northern Ireland Catholics saw themselves as an oppressed minority, while in the south the Protestant minority retained a sense of grievance at the power of the dominant Catholic majority in what for them was becoming an increasingly Catholic political ethos, if not simply a Catholic state. To many this seemed confirmed by the Constitution of 1937. The era of religious hostility with its political overtones lingered on.

Undoubtedly, the triumphalism of the centenary celebrations of Catholic Emancipation in 1929, and still more of the Eucharistic Congress in 1932, supported by high rates of Mass attendance, sacramental participation and vocations to the priesthood and religious life, fuelled for some Church leaders and members a stagnant complacency. Churchmen and political leaders enthused about Ireland's supposed destiny to lead Europe out of a spiritual Dark Ages.

A censorious approach was taken to the life of the senses generally; human existence was referred to as 'mourning and weeping in this vale of tears', as a favourite hymn put it. Sexual repression, as it is now called, was strongly associated in the public mind with religious dominance, which in turn tended to be blamed for strict state censorship of books and films. The cultural life of the nation, both in its specialist ('high') and popular forms, was impoverished. And all this was compounded by a general anti-intellectualism, widespread poverty and increasing emigration. Yet both religion (Roman Catholic style) and culture (Irish style) survived, and in some areas of thought and of activity thrived. Some of these earlier positive elements in religion and culture can be identified as harbingers of the more exciting developments of the succeeding decade.

Cultures: secular and religious

The poorly understood distinction between culture and religion, their intermingling at so many levels and in so many areas of life, from the artistic and intellectual to the political and economic, obscured what in neighbouring countries would be sharply differentiated as properly secular and properly religious. The claim by religion that it dealt with the whole of life, public and private, was actively promulgated, not least in the pages of the *Irish Ecclesiastical Record*. However, the rival secularist theory, that religion dealt with the personal and private spheres only, was not clearly or fully articulated in the decades before the 1960s. The secular claim became more actual as the decades progressed. Two notable examples of this in the early 1950s were the Mother and Child controversy, which crystallised opposition to the Church's involvement in political matters, and the extended 'Liberal Ethic' correspondence in *The Irish Times* (published as a booklet in June 1950) in which these issues were addressed explicitly and at length. In the meantime, groups such as Tuairim and earlier journals such as *The Bell*, and active publishers and writers such as Hubert Butler, were at least unconsciously preparing the ground for a more effective presentation of the secular dimensions of culture, in anticipation of the more distinctively secular culture and politics which emerged over the next decades.

Catholic print media did not fare so well in the larger market although journals such as *The Furrow* and *Doctrine and Life* (founded in the 1950s) and their older brother, *Studies,* have maintained high standards and independent stances through turbulent times.

The Catholic Church and the successes of Vatican II

The crucial religious event of the 1960s was the Vatican Council called by Pope John XXIII. Although some have subsequently criticised the Council as having gone too far, the Church would be foolish and perverse to ignore its positive and lasting contributions.

The *Declaration on Religious Freedom* was one of the last and shortest documents to be completed by Vatican II. Measured against previous Vatican statements and actions it offered radical change. Firmly based on scriptural roots, it both restored and developed the respect for human dignity and the freedom of personal and communal faith inherent, if frequently obscured, in earlier traditions. Vatican II's *Declaration* had universal implications which, if followed, would enable various churches and religions to claim their due place in any society and provide a basis in any political order for state recognition of their due freedom. Of course, it did not happen like that overnight or even over the following half-century. Ireland, in particular, retained its own complexities and obstacles, religious and political.

Another Vatican II document, the *Decree on Ecumenism,* provided an even more relevant and radical basis for resolving some of Ireland's legacy of enmity between Christians. This became increasingly significant with the onset of the Troubles in Northern Ireland. At many levels of Church life, leaders and members of the particular Christian traditions were now free to unite in prayer, preaching and practice to reject violence and to promote peace and social harmony in the midst of a mutually destructive struggle between opposing communities.

These Christian efforts may have been inadequate and the immediate impact very limited but the witness was important.

Related to the *Decree on Ecumenism* was the document on Christian dialogue with other religions and in particular with Judaism. Given Christianity's own roots and the growing understanding of the enormity of the Holocaust, especially its antecedents in Christian anti-Semitism, the Jewish dialogue was essential to the health of the Church. It had immediate impact in Ireland. Dialogue with other religions (Islam etc.) seemed much less relevant at the time, but has obviously grown in relevance since, if not in substance.

One further Vatican II document must be mentioned in the Irish social and cultural context. *Gaudium et Spes* or *The Church in the Modern World* was a serious, if at times over-optimistic, attempt to address the positive developments of the modern world and society in its various dimensions of politics, science and culture. The self-protectionism of Irish society in its dominant political, economic and cultural lives, and still more the self-enclosure of Irish Catholicism in the face of so many aspects of the modern world, were summoned beyond themselves into serious dialogue with that world. In society at large this had begun within the economic and political spheres with a new economic programme (following the adoption of *Economic Development* in 1958), moves to engage more positively with Northern Ireland and Britain and the awakening to the possibilities of both the United Nations and what was then the Common Market (which Ireland finally joined in 1973).

In Church, the rapid expansion of the missionary movement through the early 20th century had given some a sense of the wider world and its richness but did little at the time to free the home Church from its narrowness and complacency.

Although the documents just listed were in many ways the most significant for Irish society as a whole, for the self-understanding of the Church itself the dogmatic (doctrinal) *Constitution on the Church (De Ecclesia)*, usually referred to by its opening words, 'Lumen Gentium' ('The light of the nations'), is of primary importance.

This constitution stressed in particular: the role of the Church not as just another organisation, but as the sacrament or effective sign of the presence of the mystery of God in the world; the primacy of the people of God over any organisational structure; and the collegial character of the Church in all its organisational forms. These characteristics have not been notably developed in the decades since the Council, in the wider Church or in Ireland.

Some Irish cultural developments in and since the 1960s

Trying to separate religion and culture in the broadest sense is, as noted, a very difficult task. Somewhat less difficult may be distinguishing the other dimensions of that culture in its social, political, economic, educational, scientific, artistic (both popular and specialized or high), communications, entertainment and leisure dimensions. The communications and artistic dimensions have particular and somewhat neglected importance for the culture/religion interface.

Communications media

In some eastern and northern parts of Ireland, British television made an increasing impact through the 1950s. However, the spread of Irish television throughout the country following the launch of the national television service in 1961 changed significantly and irreversibly Irish social and family life. Not all such change was manifest at once. A few elements of the change took hold quickly—for example, the visual nature of news bulletins made for a much greater impact of spectacular and particularly tragic events from around the world. The Vietnam war and the Northern troubles were outstanding examples early on. Social change is more difficult to date, but undoubtedly programmes such as *The Late, Late Show* had deep impact.

The advent of Irish television and its promise persuaded the then Archbishop of Dublin, John Charles McQuaid, regarded by many as the arch-enemy of modernisation, to send two of his priests to a television training school in New York. Of course, the main persuader was the very gifted and persuasive Father Joe Dunn. Together with his fellow trainee, Father Desmond Forrestal, he went on to establish the remarkable *Radharc* series. Similar efforts by the Kairos Centre and others showed how the new media could be serious and thoughtful presenters of the Good News, which exceeded any narrow proselytising brief.

A couple of decades later, the brilliant Band Aid response to the famine in Ethiopia inspired by Irishman Bob Geldof, was a notable example of the positive value of television in bringing a whole world together. How far it would hold together in this and other contexts proved much more problematic. There is no doubt that the international television network provided a ready and valuable basis for the development of a one-world sense of the human community and eventually of the single vulnerable planet on and off which that community lived, and indeed on the one mysterious and indefinable cosmos in which it precariously existed. How profound these unities were, how well understood and how effective in action is still unproven. But some basic building blocks are to hand.

Critics argue that too often these technological and scientific achievements lead to information without understanding—in more sympathetic terms, they supply knowledge without wisdom. In Ireland the investment drive towards the 'knowledge society' has affected governments and universities at the expense of the great educational ideals of the development of the whole human being. These losses have been aggravated by close ties of much scientific and technological progress with financial and commercial success.

The ignoring of the imaginative dimensions of the human mind in social relations, and of the philosophical discipline of ethics in the whole range of human activity, has left a huge void in social life. We have seen recently the cost of reducing the criteria for political progress and human development to economic achievement—a spectacular disaster, not caused by technological incompetence, but by neglect of the humanities in education and application. The current debate on university education initiated by Professor Tom Garvin[1] exposes the problem effectively, although his position is hotly contested by some respondents. As I have addressed the same problem more fully in some recent publications,[2] I will not pursue it further here.

In a different mode, the advances in interpersonal communication, whether, for example, by mobile phone or e-mail, have their own negativities. It would be foolish to deny the immense potential of both in maintaining genuine human contact between family members and

1 In *The Irish Times*, Saturday, 2 May 2010

2 *Theology in Winter Light* (Dublin, 2010) *Immersed in Mystery* (Dublin, 2007)

friends who are separated geographically. On the social and political side it has brought new opportunities to impoverished and oppressed peoples in finding support and help across many divides. But there are the inevitable down-sides. Mobile phones, for all their convenience, can and do become utter distractions both from any work that requires personal concentration and from the necessary quiet time that everybody needs for mental and spiritual health. Of course, we live in an already noisy and distracting environment, but the mobile phone adds a new inner dimension of noise to the already perturbed ear. Similarly, while e-mail has its obvious consolations and liberating effects, it does leave one vulnerable to a procession of commercial junk and more objectionable material. As with all technological advances the user must remain in charge.

Artistic achievement: theatre and poetry

Support in face of such threats is available through the achievements of good artists at both the 'higher' and 'popular' levels. There has been a remarkable revolution in almost all areas of the arts since the late 1950s and early 1960s, a revolution still in need of some overall mapping and analysis.

Musicians, painters, sculptors and architects as well as poets, playwrights and fiction writers developed new energies and insights. How far these developments were facilitated by a new openness to the world, and the beginnings of a new domestic liberalism and prosperity, is difficult to determine. Perhaps there was a set of mutual influences at work which enabled the various dimensions of Irish society to liberate one another. I will address theatre and poetry as emblematic and then only through a few examples from each.

Perhaps harking to an earlier theatrical tradition such as the disturbances in the Abbey on the first nights of Synge's *Playboy of the Western World*, the early signs of new life in the theatre were those of serious objections and controversy. The 1957 prosecution of the Pike production of Tennessee Williams' *The Rose Tattoo* (there was alleged to have been a condom on stage), the response to the 1958 refusal by the then Archbishop of Dublin to sanction a play by O'Casey and an adaptation of *Ulysses* planned for the Tóstal festival, and the 1959 Belfast controversy about Sam Thompson's *Over the Bridge* did indicate some fresh life after a rather stagnant period. More positively Brendan Behan's *The Quare Fellow* (1954) and Samuel Beckett's *Waiting for Godot* (1955), both produced at the Pike, heralded a really new era in Irish theatre. Fertile ground for such developments had been prepared by the thriving amateur dramatic societies spread all over the country and their now annual climax at the Athlone Festival.

The home-based theatre revolutionaries of the 1960s included Brian Friel, Tom Murphy and Tom Kilroy, all three of them happily still writing. While Beckett becomes the ghost in the wings asking ultimate questions about the point/futility of human existence, for so many of the new playwrights their first offerings dealt directly with more immediate and hitherto suppressed problems of contemporary and recognizable Irish people. Two of the breakthrough plays, Murphy's *A Whistle in the Dark* (first produced in London in 1961 having been rejected earlier by the Abbey) and Friel's *Philadelphia Here I Come!* (1964) dealt with the great scourge of emigration as well as revealing some deeper ills of human relations in Irish society.

In *Philadelphia,* which focuses on the agonising and ambivalence of a would-be emigrant and his almost empty relationship with his father, Friel employs the device of the Public Gar and Private Gar to convey the ambivalence of the younger man. Murphy deals with the family of emigrants already settled in Britain and then with that frequently ignored and unnamed internal family violence, especially among men. One of Kilroy's early plays, *The Death and Resurrection of Mr Roche* (1968) dealt with latent homosexuality, still a difficult subject in those years.

Of course, the range of fresh subject matter was not the only or even the most significant achievement of these 1960s plays. Their character-drawing, dramatic sense, storytelling ability, stagecraft and ear for dialogue were highly developed. In Friel's case, these gifts were crowned by lyrical language and psychological subtlety. In Murphy, the sheer power of *A Whistle in the Dark* and later works was both terrifying and exhilarating. Kilroy was sometimes less ambitious but never short of innovation in story and character. In his latest play, *Christ Deliver Us* (2010), he adapts (radically) a late 19th-century German piece to 20th-century Ireland and confronts physical abuse in boarding schools and the accompanying difficulties of teenage sex, pregnancy and suicide. Such a crude summary makes the play sound much less persuasive than it is on stage, although it has a certain element of melodrama about it which Kilroy tends to share with Murphy, and in this case may be influenced by the original German play.

The decades subsequent to the 1960s witnessed a new golden age of Irish theatre with new and serious playwrights joining the original trio, new companies like Druid (Galway), Field Day (Derry), Charabanc (Belfast) and Rough Magic (Dublin). Outstanding among the new playwrights are, in my opinion, Sebastian Barry and Marina Carr, although one dare not ignore the achievements of Frank McGuinness. Marie Jones, Stuart Parker, Martin McDonagh and Conor McPherson.

The poets offer an even more bewildering richness in two languages and from all parts of Ireland, as well as significant translations from the wider worlds of poetry. That wayward and influential genius, Patrick Kavanagh, carried on from the 1950s, but many of the great names only began publishing in the 1960s, for example, Derek Mahon, Seamus Heaney and Michael Longley, near contemporaries like Thomas Kinsella and John Montague, with Paul Durcan and Eavan Boland shortly afterwards. Poetry in the Irish language heralded by Seán Ó Ríordáin and Máirtín Ó Direáin found new voices in Michael Hartnett, Nuala Ní Dhomhnaill, Michael Davitt and numerous others.

In his recent collection, *Life is a Dream: 40 Years Reading Poems, 1967–2007*, Paul Durcan provides an appropriate starting point for exploring this contribution. Poetry readings by a range of poets became one of the cultural highlights of the last decades. In his readings, Durcan offers a one-man poetic-dramatic performance. This is true of the broad range of his poetic subjects, from his satirical exposures of the tragic silliness of Irish life in such poems as 'Celtic Tiger', to the love poems for his separated wife, Nessa, and the celebration of his daughter Sarah's wedding in Rakestreet, Mayo to his affectionate elegies for friends now gone, to his complex reflections on his father and mother to his insightful poems on the Northern Troubles such as 'In Memory: the Miami Showband—massacred 31 July 1975' and 'Omagh'. In truth, there is scarcely a significant facet or face of Irish society which Durcan does not humanise and enrich by his joy and sorrow, his laughter and tears, his mockery and appreciation during these forty years.

The humanising and enrichment are a feature of all the many good poets of the era. Women poets have become more prominent and cherished. Kerry Hardie's 'Ship of Death' from her 1996 collection *A Furious Place* illustrates an aspect of life which transcends economics, technology and even science, the whole gamut of the 'successful' knowledge society.

> *Watching you for the first time,*
> *turn to prepare your boat, my mother;*
> *making it clear you have other business now—*
> *the business of your future—*

In that balancing of person and society which appeared to be devoured by the Celtic Tiger, the many human languages play a significant role. Notable is the present thriving of Irish language or Gaelic poetry. In contemporary Irish poetry poetic translations from a host of other languages are a continuing and joyful surprise.

Church and culture since the 1960s: some Irish interactions

1. The fall of the faith professions

The decline of deference and trust in our society has been noted by many commentators. The wide-ranging scandals in politics, in property, in banking and especially in the Church have significantly changed people's attitudes. A recent survey by the market research company, Amárach[3] charted the collapse of trust in the major institutions in the state over the decades. These included the gamut of what I might call the faith professions: the government, the media, the Church, the banks, the health service and the legal profession. The public are struggling to assess the full extent of the increase in distrust and the rapidity with which it happened. To appreciate the social impact of all this it is necessary to be aware of the trust and prestige which all of these professions and institutions enjoyed for so long in Irish society.

The crucial value of trust must pervade every personal, social and economic relationship. Trust cuts deeply into every person's life from womb to tomb. As the person matures though childhood into adolescence, adulthood, old age, the contexts will change but the need for trust and the destructiveness of trust-betrayed persist. At the heart of trust is self-entrusting to the other, the stranger, from the stranger-

3 Published in February, 2010

parent of the new-born babe to the professional but still stranger—carer of the ill, the aged and the dying. Such self-entrusting ramifies through every dimension of human living. Its evident and pervasive betrayal in our current society reaches deeply and painfully into all aspects of human life.

The foundation of such human trusting is not easy. Need does not provide a satisfying final explanation. Ultimately one has to make an act of faith in the 'faith professional' with whom one is immediately dealing in one's need. The effective operation of the professions—priests, doctors, lawyers, bankers, politicians, journalists etc.—is completely dependent on the trust or faith of their constituents, clients, patients, parishioners, readers and audiences. The decline in faith in all such professionals will require for its recovery in human terms a radical renewal of these professions and the slow healing that leads from distrust and cynicism to fresh trust and faith without any final human guarantee against further betrayal.

The faith/trust unity, whether directed to the human or divine, finds meaningful expression in a range of languages, actions, relationships and institutions. Verbal commitments such as marriage vows, medical directives or legal instruments voice commitment in words and bind in trust their adherents. As language itself changes and circumstances are seriously altered over the ages, the true meaning and intent of such professions may require fresh interpretation and commitment.

In Christian theological contexts that phenomenon of re-interpretation (described as 'development of doctrine') has frequently led to serious divisions among believers. In the current Church such divisions focus on the correct understanding of Vatican II and on the weight given to issues of continuity and discontinuity at that Council. Hard words about implementation and non-implementation are rife. This distrust generated between the divided groups damages the community of believers, which as a result is always in need of healing. In the search for ultimates, for faith in the apparent void, hope against despair and trust beyond ultimate betrayal, the religious believer finds anchor in God. On the model of Jesus Christ he or she is enabled to move beyond the abandonment on Calvary to Jesus' commending of his Spirit to that God.

2. Communications, the news media and the Good News
In one of the many ironies of this 'most distrustful country', aware-

ness of the widespread distrust of the professions is mainly due to the publicity given to their failures in the communications media, in print, on the radio and television. Yet, according to the Amárach survey, these very media themselves score highly in the distrust ratings. Distrust of them is partly accounted for by the misleading headlines, biased reporting and poorly considered editorial stances of which they are regularly guilty. Worse, however, especially in print media, is the domination of comment and opinion over regular and reliable news reporting. All these difficulties are exacerbated by fierce competition between the various outlets, in which the judgment or lack of it by journalists appears to be rewarded by readers and viewers. There has developed therefore a media culture which is strong in exposure of the failures of others but with little acknowledgment of its own failures and fallibilities. In another irony, in this the media mimics the activity in the past of so many national institutions of which the media is deeply critical, especially the Church.

It should be acknowledged that in the last couple of years the Catholic Church has made valiant if belated efforts to admit its serious failures. By putting in place prevention measures, at least in regard to clerical child abuse, and making some efforts at repentance through resignations and restitution, it has begun to prepare for the renewal of its primary task of authentic preaching and saving ministry. It still has a long journey ahead in retrieving a truly Gospel position

3. Sacred and secular

Vatican II's *Declaration on Religious Freedom* and elements of its *Constitution on the Church in the Modern World* were taken by the faithful as the latest developments in the positive and mutually enriching distinguishing of sacred and secular. They emerged at the end of a long and mostly hostile struggle between forces that had, well into the 20th century, sought to subdue or even eliminate the secular opposition. That struggle marks the 21st century as religious powers of various origins, notably Muslim, but including far-right Christian groups, promote the dominance of the sacred. Meanwhile secular forces hold still to Voltaire's *'écrasez l'infame'* led by such Western spokespeople as Richard Dawkins.

The opposing forces may be less shrill in Ireland but they are undoubtedly at work, as many recent debates and discussions have revealed. The idea of banishing religion from the 'public square', as it is sometimes called, has many influential advocates, particularly in the aftermath of the recent Church scandals. A strong resistance to such a move is also evident.

The spiritual dimension

I shall continue my concentration on theatre and poetry: other artistic forms such as painting, sculpture and music from artists such as Imogen Stuart, Patrick Pye, Hughie O'Donoghue, Seán Ó Riada and Ronan McDonagh—the broader spiritual reference of such artists must be largely ignored here. Happily there is a thoughtful survey of much of this in *Underground Cathedrals* by Mark Patrick Hederman, Abbot of Glenstal,[4] home of Michael Sweetman's old school.

The formally religious work of such poets and dramatists as John F. Deane, Pádraig Daly, Paul Murray, Desmond Forrestal and Pat O'Brien must also be taken for granted here although it is an important signpost to the religious-cultural interaction of the period. In the broader, what one might term loosely the 'Kandinsky', sense of the spiritual dimension of the arts, many poets and playwrights have exposed the deeper dimensions of nature and humanity in ways that verge on the transcendent or religious whether they intend to or not, mostly not. This is adverted to in Dennis O'Driscoll's insightful poem, 'Missing God'.

The majority of the good poems and plays of the last half-century touch on the depth dimension which Wassily Kandinsky in this context labelled the spiritual. It would be difficult to read Heaney or Kinsella, Boland or Ní Dhomhnaill, watch Beckett, Friel or Murphy, without being liberated into a fuller humanity, without being taken well beyond or deeply within oneself. The 'beyond' and 'within' offer space for dialogue with all the great questions which confront us but are largely ignored in the otherwise vacuous context of so much of our daily lives. The leading British theatre critic, Michael Billington, wrote recently that issues raised by religion badly needed expression on stage, because of the emptiness of so much public discourse.[5] Our best poets and playwrights offer a platform for the rehearsal of the

4 Published by Columba Press (Dublin 2010)

5 In *The Guardian*, 21 May 2010

basic ultimate or religious questions, which otherwise find it so hard to get a hearing.

The very secularity of some of these works sweeps away the trivia of religious thought, language and practice and allows a purer and renewed religious awareness to be gradually awakened. That will take time and effort and continuing education. Yet the groundwork has been laid for us by these artists as we seek to understand and live the Good News anew. Herein lie some of the missing links in our current culture and religion dialogue.

Triumph and disaster: recent stories of Irish society and Church

The question today for Church and society in Ireland is one of survival. Can a new vision of 'What is Catholic or Irish?' emerge from the current crises? The triumphalist, hierarchical Church has been dragged down by the clerical/paedophile crises to humiliating levels. In the melée the values of Vatican II have been gradually eclipsed. Can the positive relationships with the world and secular culture which appeared to be developing in the Catholic Church during the Council survive? The question is, after due repentance and restructuring, can the real church of Christ's disciples be freed to enter again into dialogue and partnership with other religions and a renewed wider democratic society of equality, integrity and prosperity? This is what the best of the Catholic political and cultural and indeed religious thinkers and activists like Michael Sweetman were seeking in the 1960s for Irish society and so, at least implicitly, for Irish church.

The unfinished Temple of the Spirit: human and divine

Dom Mark Patrick Hederman's reference to the underground cathedrals obviously embraces dwelling places of the human and divine spirit. It might also be recognized as the unfinished cathedral echoing the extended building and rebuilding of the great medieval cathedrals and still more akin to the deliberate unfinished approach of Gaudi in building the modern cathedral in Barcelona. Only very recently have we begun to observe the death throes of 'Constantinian' and feudal Church structures as we have known them since the Council of Trent, long after they have disappeared in Western political society. In

Christian belief, 'unfinished in history' is an essential element of the Temple of the Holy Spirit in its divine and human dimensions. The work in progress characteristic of Christian living and community applies in its own way to individual and communal artistic labours, so the dialogue can and must go on.

The unfinished life of Michael Sweetman

Despite the tragic curtailment of Michael Sweetman's historical life he lives on even in historical embodiment through his widow and children, their memories and those of his friends. There will always be Sweetman-Becker genes deriving from the married life and family of Michael and Barbara. His bereaved family will also ensure the further life of his ideals and ideas. This is naturally most evident in the subsequent commitments and causes which Barbara pursued. At the ultimate spiritual and Christian level Michael lives on in the communion of the living and the dead, the communion of saints, of which the risen Christ is the symbol and realisation.

The father I hardly knew

Timothy Sweetman

I find it somewhat strange to be asked for my memories of my father, a man I hardly remember.

I have snippets, of course, like him pulling up his trousers as he sat down, or of looking up at him when I was playing with a farmyard set in the big room in my grandparents' Donegal holiday home.

He must have been there, I suppose, when we went with the architect (I think) to discuss 'modifications' to the warren of small rooms at the back of 20 Park Drive, the Dream House my parents had bought and had only finished renovating shortly before his death. One of the clear memories I do have is of him throwing me up in the air (I was a lot thinner then) in the resulting kitchen with its lemon-yellow floor, and catching me, me laughing all the time.

My other main memory is going around the polling stations for what, looking back, must have been the 1972 referendum on joining the EEC. We were stuck in traffic a few hundred metres from one of the stations in Finglas when, in a fit of impatience, he pulled up onto the (wide) pavement and drove along. I'm beginning to think driving skills are genetic.

Mum told me once that I used to pester her about the crash and the reasons for it. I have a strong memory of one such occasion at the kitchen sink and vague memories of other occasions. I suppose I was trying to figure out what had happened without realising the pain I was unintentionally inflicting. Mum tells me that I used to ask why we didn't all go to heaven to be with Daddy. I think they always ended with that awful, unanswerable, question 'But *why*, Mummy?'

I've often in the past asked myself, what would have happened if he'd lived? The more general areas of economics and politics I think are covered elsewhere in this book by people better qualified than I. But I suppose I've wondered what the impact might have been on the family and on me. Would I have made different choices at that crucial school-leaving age as one starts out in life? Would I have been more clued-in about what I wanted to do? Would I have still gone to university or done some more vocationally-based training? Would he have given me the necessary boot up the backside I so urgently needed? Possibly. Another thoroughly unanswerable question.

I have of course heard stories of what he was like and the energy he had. The sheer breadth of his interests and activities always makes me feel inadequate. Family, politics, economics, business, farming, the list seems endless. I never really knew him obviously; but he's a father I can be proud of, and love, and miss.

A life in pictures

MS in 1935, as a baby with his mother

MS with his brother David, in the pram

MS aged 4, smart with his gloves in his hand

With the lads at school in St Gerard's, Co. Wicklow (l–r) John Oliver Sweetman (cousin), John Dillon (cousin), MS, his brother David and George Moorhead, a friend and neighbour from Co Meath

On holiday in the West of Ireland—with the family's Siamese cats.
Front (l–r) MS, David, Elizabeth, his mother and father.
Back (l–r) Mary, Kate and Margaret

Barbara and MS signing the marriage register 5 March 1957

With the twins Caroline and Michèle in Montreal; MS is holding Michèle

With Rachel at a ruin in Co Meath

This photograph appeared in the New York Advocate *in June 1963, with the following caption: 'Mr Michael Sweetman accompanied by his wife and family are shown as they board an Irish International Airlines Shamrock Jet en route for Dublin, Ireland. Mr Sweetman returned to Ireland after finishing his two year assignment as Manager, North America, of the Irish Trade Board. From left to right: Patrick, age 4; Mr Michael Sweetman holding baby Christopher, age 2; Caroline and Michèle, twins aged 5½ and Mrs Michael Sweetman.'*

With Patrick, Rachel, Christopher and Michèle

The gate of Johnsbrook drawn by his sister-in-law Margaret Becker

Fishing with his father Paddy in Donegal

On the fruit farm

A happy family snap, which turned out to be
the last photo taken of MS and his children,
in May 1972. MS has his hands on Timmy's
shoulders.

MS watches while Guy Jackson, President of the Federation of Irish Industries, presents the first edition of Challenge *to George Colley TD Minister for Industry and Commerce in 1968*

The Federation of Irish Industries deputation which discussed price control with George Colley, the Minister for Industry and Commerce, in 1967. Front (l–r) Bernard Roche, Finbarr Ambrose, Sydney Gibson (President FII), Guy Jackson (Director General FII), James Stacey. Back (l–r) Joe Manahan, Bill Brosnan, Brendan Cassidy and MS.

The Irish Times' *front page announcement of the fatal air crash on 18 June 1972 that took the lives of MS, eleven leading Irish businessmen and 106 other passengers as their Trident on the way to Brussels crashed at Staines a few miles outside Heathrow.*

Writings by
Michael Sweetman

The Common Name of Irishman[1]

Michael Sweetman

In the short time in which we, as a group of people working for peace in Northern Ireland, got to know Michael Sweetman, we found a person who rose above party politics. His sincerity and compassion was to be seen in everything he did and said and his concern for his fellow-man was shown in a practical way. It is with deep regret that all of us who were associated with him learned of his untimely death. Ireland, North and South, will be poorer for his passing.

The present pamphlet by the New Ulster Movement[2] ends with this question (addressed on behalf of Northern Unionism to 'the South'): 'Provided a just restructuring can be achieved in the North, would it not be better for all of us if you went your way and we went ours—two States acknowledging their different traditions, but ready to cooperate in all matters of common concern?' It is fair that this question should be put.

The pamphlet does not make a convincing case that the 'two-State' solution is the best or indeed even a possible solution. Equally, of course, in the Republic, advocates of 'national unity' have not usually made a convincing case either, as Dennis Kennedy so tellingly illustrated in his articles in *The Irish Times* some months ago. In a curious way both sides seem to be trying to prop up with reasonable arguments attitudes which basically defy rational explanation.

The problem we face is the creation of an Ireland which every Irishman can accept. We have to embark on that search without preconceptions about political or constitutional structures. Political structures exist to convenience people—they are not things with an

1 An uncorrected draft of this pamphlet was published in Belfast on 24 June 1972 by Michael's friends, at the request of Barbara Sweetman. The author had planned to add a section on 'The South'.

2 *Two Irelands or One?*, (May 1972). Belfast: New Ulster Movement

independent existence to which people must be subordinated.

The NUM proposition implied in the quoted sentence has a superficial plausibility. There are, in a sense, two 'nations' in Ireland. In the abstract one can define them quite readily according to widely accepted stereotypes. One is Catholic, vaguely Gaelic in origin, instinctively anti-British and with its focal point in the southern part of the country. The other is Protestant, of vaguely British origin, generally pro-British in attitude and centred in the Northern part of the country. It would, of course, be the most logical and convenient solution to our problems if these two supposedly incompatible 'nations' could neatly divide the country between them and, as NUM says, go their own way as friends.

The trouble is that a nation is an abstract idea. It cannot readily be given concrete form and measurable dimensions. More than fifty million people died violently in Europe this century because some people, most notably Hitler, thought it could. People are dying in Ireland today because of the same misconception. Our problem is that while in the abstract, we are two 'nations', most individual Irish men and women cannot, in practice, be so readily categorised, labelled and assigned to one or other. True, that there are typical Southern Catholic 'Gaels' and typical Northern Protestant Unionists, but such pure samples are a minority of the total population of the island—the vast majority of us are a mongrel lot, coming in all conceivable colours, shapes and sizes. The task of separating out this country in a physical sense into two political and social entities, to conform to the two abstract 'nations' which we recognise, would be about as easy as to separate out in the individual Irishman the Gaelic, the Norman, the English, the Scottish, the Viking, the Huguenot, the Spanish.

The weakness of the NUM case is that it does not grasp this basic problem. Our troubles are due at least as much to a misguided effort over the past fifty years to create two such separate entities as they are due to equally misguided attempts to impose on the whole people of Ireland a social and political framework based on a grossly oversimplified unitary view of our true racial and cultural heritage.

'Is it not true', the NUM asks, 'that the most practical reason why you (i.e. the South) have so far supported a united Ireland is that it seemed the only means of securing justice for the minority in the North?'. No, it is not true. In fact, to its shame, the South's interest in justice in the North up to the start of the civil rights movement in 1968 was minimal. All the emphasis in anti-partitionist propaganda was instead on 'our claim' to the full national territory. There is no evidence that anti-partitionism was much concerned with the practical welfare of the people of Northern Ireland, majority or minority. It was concerned rather with abstracts like national aims and historic destinies.

I do not recall any anti-partitionist putting forward a convincing case that the majority of people North or South would benefit in a practical, tangible way from the removal of the Border. Instead, the argument was at an almost mystical level on these lines: 'All the Nation's ills are due to suppression of the Irish nation by Britain. Gain political independence and all the political, economic and social problems, which are caused by lack of independence, will be solved. But independence for the 26 counties didn't solve these problems. Therefore it was not true independence. True independence must include the 32 counties. Then the problems would be solved.' Here we are in the realm of pure faith because it was never clear how the addition of the Six Counties to the Twenty Six could help to solve such problems as economic underdevelopment, emigration, unemployment, poor housing, poor education . . . Looked at without the eye of faith, such a move was most likely merely to bring the Six Counties down towards the Twenty Six County level.

It is easy to demolish this anti-partitionist nonsense but the basic fact remains that most people North and South know in their hearts that while we may be two 'nations', we are in a very real sense one people. On this point the NUM pamphlet shows muddled thinking. 'Southerners still seem generally to assume that the island of Ireland is the national unit in this part of Europe, and that everyone living on it should automatically feel his first loyalty towards Ireland . . . Southerners must face the fact that, to a large majority in Northern Ireland, British nationality seems as natural as the air they breathe.' Even if the latter statement were in fact true (which is arguable in the light of recent events) it is a basic misconception to regard 'loyalty towards Ireland' as incompatible with feelings of 'British nationality', defined in the pamphlet as a tradition of service in the British forces or public service and a general identification with the English speaking world. For as the pamphlet itself points out, this dual position is equally true of many Catholics in Northern Ireland, and, it might have added, of many Catholics and Protestants who are fully loyal citizens of the Republic. In reality, these traditions are not incompatible with loyalty towards Ireland, which is felt equally by Northerners and Southerners, but with a particular concept of the Irish nation (Catholic, Gaelic, anti-British, inward looking) which, although through a twist of historic circumstances it has been official orthodoxy in the South for the best part of fifty years, has never genuinely been accepted by a majority of people North or South in any real sense. Do the vast majority of the citizens of Dublin show any genuine aspiration to become 'Gaelic'. Or, at the real life level as opposed to the level of political theory, are they really anti-British? Do they refuse to watch British television or listen to British radio, reject British tastes and goods, refuse to work in Britain, avoid marrying or being friends with British people? Most people in the South know perfectly well that in real everyday life they are just as much involved with Britain and the rest of the English speaking world as any Northern Protestant.

The hysterical 'Britishness' of many Northerners—Union-Jack-waving, God-Save-the-Queen-singing, to a degree that perplexes every visiting Englishman, has less to do with feelings of British nationality than with political factionalism in a purely Irish context. Equally the tricolour-waving, Soldier Song-singing, decade-of-the-rosary-in-Irish-reciting groups don't reflect a love of Ireland or of religion so much as the assertion of a particular brand of nationalism.

'Irish nationalism' and 'loyalty to Ireland' are not the same thing, although Southern Catholic Republicans have often tried to make us believe that they were. Many Irish people for personal or family reasons feel a simultaneous attachment to several different counties of Ireland. To force us to make absolute choices between supposed incompatibilities when in fact such choices are not really necessary is merely part of the simplifying fanaticism of nationalism—a hangover from an Anglo-Irish conflict situation of the past. One does not have to choose between loving Wicklow or Kerry if one in fact happens to love both. One can feel close kinship with Britain without being disloyal to Ireland, just as one can believe in European unity and yet remain fully an Irishman.

In another part of the pamphlet the NUM seems closer to understanding this when it talks about finding ways in a united Ireland of 'conciliating the British sentiments of the minority'. Certainly some symbolic gestures of the kind mentioned, such as rejoining the Commonwealth, might be needed to symbolise a real change of attitude in the new State, but this problem can be met only by a full acceptance throughout Irish society of the validity of an Irishness beyond the narrow definitions imposed by Catholic nationalism.

Here the NUM's remarks on the 'cult of physical force' are relevant, but oversimplified. The vast majority of Irish people south of the border do not subscribe to a cult of physical force. Whenever they have had an opportunity of saying so they have said so with extraordinary decisiveness, whether in the derisory support given to physical force advocates at elections or in the massive majority in the recent referendum whose scale clearly owed much to an almost universal rejection of their espousal of the anti-EEC cause. It is, of course, true that events in the early part of this century, accentuated by the incompetence and chicanery of Westminster politicians and influenced by the impact on this country of romantic nationalist mythology, led to a division between two extremist factions, the Green nationalists of the South and the Orange nationalists of the North. As is inevitable in such situations the ordinary man was forced to take sides, to choose between one faction or the other—the same kind of polarisation as has taken place within Northern Ireland recently. Inevitably the vast majority in the South, when forced to choose, chose the Green side, and since the 1920s political survival in Southern society has required lip service to the 'heroes' and 'heroic events' of the Green faction. But as the partisans immediately involved disappear from the scene, so too the potency of the old totems is ebbing away. 1916 or 1921 do not stir the twenty-year-olds of today as they did those of a generation ago. The 'cult of physical force' is not a fundamental part of Southern culture, society or outlook; it is an increasingly meaningless symbolism based on the factionalism of the past.

The NUM is perfectly right when it says 'There is no prospect of building a united Ireland on an anti-British basis'. One of the real arguments for a United Ireland is that by healing the division caused by the polarised factions, it would make irrelevant the display of either side's party symbols.

Unity is above all the cause of those who do not want to identify with either faction, because they recognise that each faction has appropriated and perverted one part of a heritage which we all share—a heritage which is as indivisible as a human personality.

That is not to say that the solution is simply to absorb the present Six Counties into the Twenty Six. Far from it. It is merely to say that the problem which underlies the present tragedy in Northern Ireland is one which it is the responsibility of the inhabitants of the whole island to solve, because it follows from the history which all of us share equally, not just from the history or circumstances of Northern Ireland in isolation. Meaningful unity means, first of all, full acceptance of that responsibility by the partisans of both nationalisms and a readiness without preconceptions to devise together a political, social and economic framework which will allow all of us on this island to live together in peace.

From the Northerners' point of view there is now an immediate and practical case for an accommodation with the Republic. Most people in Northern Ireland, whether Protestant or Catholic, want self-government and most Protestants were content with the form of self-government which they had under the old Stormont system. The former Unionist now faces a very difficult choice—a choice between self-determination which must be based on reconciliation and co-operation with the Green faction, or some form of Westminster rule, whether it be full integration with the United Kingdom or indefinite continuance of the present arrangements. Faced with that choice a majority of people in Northern Ireland would choose self-determination (and I believe even a majority of Protestants would so choose).

But the reconciliation of the factions—a precondition of a successful self-determination solution—could not be limited to Northern Ireland only. It must inevitably involve a settlement in the whole country of what is essentially the same feud. Dreams of self-determination à la Vanguard[3] are nonsense, as most Northerners know in their hearts. Economically, politically, militarily a UDI[4] revolt could not succeed against the combined hostility of the Irish and British Governments. Self-determination for Ulster is possible only with the

3 Vanguard, which originated in 1972 as a right-wing pressure group inside the Ulster Unionist Party, proposed independence for Northern Ireland inside a 'community of the British Isles'.

4 The concept of a Unilateral Declaration of Independence (UDI) entered political discourse with the actions of Ian Smith and the government of Rhodesia in 1965

consent of both governments. That consent will be given only in certain conditions which must necessarily include a general Irish settlement. It is not only the vast majority of Irishmen who want this feud settled once and for all—Britain too has had more than a bellyful of the Irish question.

What kind of settlement would be fair to both factions in Ulster and to the people of Ireland generally?

The key point in such a settlement must be the freely-given consent of both communities in Northern Ireland. It is not, however, a question of presenting some new constitutional scheme in a referendum and asking for a 'yes' or 'no' decision. Consent will have to evolve just as new attitudes and new institutions will have to evolve which will not spring fully grown from some super-conference. When the talking starts it must first be about smaller immediate things on which agreement is possible. This is a time when too much argument about ultimate destinations must be avoided. The thing is to get moving, however slowly—we can decide what turn to take at the various crossroads when we come to them.

It is my contention that evolving consent can be achieved only in the context of a renewal of self-government in Northern Ireland. No major change should be made in the constitutional position of Northern Ireland, either in relation to Britain or in relation to the Republic until Northern Ireland has achieved a sufficient level of self-government to participate through democratic institutions in any such decision.

What are the alternatives to this approach? Leaving on one side the clearly unacceptable alternative of an indefinite continuation of the present situation, there are three other possibilities:

(i) Full integration of Northern Ireland into the United Kingdom,
(ii) Full integration into the Republic,
(iii) UDI.

Full integration into the United Kingdom

This is a non-starter because neither the present British Government nor the Labour Party would consider it. While full integration might solve short-term problems particularly by removing civil rights grievances, it would leave the British Government again sitting on an

Irish time-bomb with the ever-present danger of violent nationalism re-emerging. Full integration would not solve the Irish question for Britain, it would merely brush it under the carpet again. In any case, it is doubtful whether a majority of Protestants in Northern Ireland want full integration. Their position would, of course, depend on the alternatives being offered. If the only alternative were absorption into the Republic in its present form then almost certainly a majority of Protestants would opt for integration into the UK. But it would be widely regarded as the lesser of two very definite evils.

Integration into the Republic

The British Government is committed to holding a plebiscite in Northern Ireland on whether or not this solution is acceptable. Now or in the future the proposal is likely to be defeated by a substantial majority if framed as a simple yes or no to 'national unity' in the traditional sense. Even if the British Government were prepared to renege on its commitment and force the Northern majority into a united Ireland against its will, it would be disastrous for the Government of the Republic to be a party to such a transaction. Forcing the Northern majority into a united Ireland in a sullen and defiant mood might relieve the British Government of a problem of which it had grown weary—it would not solve the real problem within Ireland.

The traditional nationalist view—reiterated recently in Mr McManus' pamphlet[5]—that if Britain 'got out' the problem could then be solved by the Irish themselves is a euphemistic way of saying that if the Green faction were left a clear field, they would soon force the Northern Protestant to accept the Green concept of Ireland. This faction, of course, has its precise equivalent on the other side in Northern Ireland in those Protestants who believe that if all Catholics were either killed or driven out, or cowed into abject submission, there would no longer be any problem in Northern Ireland.

Even if for some wholly unexpected reason a majority voted 'Yes' in a plebiscite, (made up of the Catholic population plus a minority of Protestants) immediate incorporation of Northern Ireland into the

5 Frank McManus was nationalist MP for Fermanagh South Tyrone 1970-74. His pamphlet *Ulster the future* (1972) supported the Eire Nua idea of a federal solution for Ireland including a parliament for a nine-county Ulster.

Republic would not be desirable. A simple majority in Northern Ireland in favour of this would not necessarily mean that the communal problem within Northern Ireland had been solved, and if it had not, there is no reason to think that incorporation into the Republic would do anything other than intensify it.

UDI

Talk of UDI is an emotional response to the suspension of Stormont and has been used by some Northern political leaders to give some kind of shadowy rationale to Vanguard/UDA type activity. Even the most obvious implications and problems of UDI have not been publicly explored. It does not in fact stand up to serious examination. Firstly, it is economically impossible. Not only is the whole structure of Northern Ireland's economy and standard of living under-pinned by British subsidy—most of its trade is also with Britain. Even if one imagines an extreme Protestant movement winning sufficient political and military power in Northern Ireland to declare it independent, Britain is thus in a position immediately to bring about its total economic collapse. One has to assume that any such unilateral declaration of independence would be opposed both by Westminster and Dublin. The two Governments between them are in a position to make UDI economically impossible.

There is another insuperable obstacle to successful UDI. The vast majority of Northern Catholics would oppose bitterly the establishment of an avowedly Protestant sectarian state which would certainly be even less tolerant than Stormont at its worst. If Stormont was made unworkable because the minority were no longer prepared to accept it, a UDI situation would be vastly more difficult to maintain, beset as it would be by severe economic difficulties, with no support from the British Government and presumably with the British army against it.

The UDI movement is important not because it has any chance of success but because the sentiment in favour of it amongst some Northern Protestants reflects a real urge for self-determination in the Protestant community. It underlines how little real support there is in Northern Ireland for complete integration into the United Kingdom. It reveals what has never before been openly admitted, that 'loyalism' is simply a form of Orange Sinn Féin. In a sense, the UDI movement can be said to represent a political advance in that almost all significant political groups in Ireland, North and South, are now on common ground of wanting some form of political independence for Ireland. It can be said that the argument in Northern Ireland is no longer about whether the whole of Ireland should be independent or not; it is really about what kind of independent Ireland it should be.

9-County Ulster?

Before developing these points further one other suggestion must, however, be considered. A proposal for some form of regional government in Northern Ireland covering all nine counties of Ulster is being increasingly canvassed, most recently in a pamphlet by Mr Frank McManus MP. It has some superficial attraction but when examined in more detail the idea presents basic difficulties.

Would the people of Cavan, Monaghan and Donegal want to move out of the Republic and in to a new Northern State? How big a majority in the three counties would be required to justify changing their status in this way?

What purpose would be served anyway by enlarging Northern Ireland in this way? Increased economic viability? But the three counties concerned would not be much help here—indeed arguably they could be an added burden on Northern Ireland. Geographically more logical? In the case of Donegal perhaps yes, but would a border drawn between Meath and Cavan or Louth and Monaghan be geographically any more logical or convenient than the present border?

On the other hand, one notes that the three counties concerned were excluded from the original settlement of 1920 because their inclusion would have risked a Catholic nationalist majority in Northern Ireland. Could it be—unworthy thought—that the real motive behind the nine-county Ulster idea is to convert the present Northern majority into a Northern minority? This suspicion is reinforced by the fact that the nine-county Ulster proposal has been most vigorously promoted by the most blatantly sectarian of the Republican groups—the Provisionals. It would be particularly advantageous from their point of view in possibly giving control of Northern Ireland to Northern Catholics—whom they hope to lead—without their having in turn to submit to an All-Ireland state in which they would be an even smaller minority than the Northern Unionists. As Frank McManus points out in his pamphlet, there is often less in common between Catholics from Kerry and Belfast than there is between Northern Catholics and Protestants. But this also means—and the referendum underlined this—that Northern Republicans of the Provisional type might not find an all-Ireland climate very congenial.

The simple answer to the nine-county Ulster proposition is that if there is a case for that, there is just as good a case for giving the same kind of autonomy to the present Six Counties.

Re-establishment of a Northern Ireland Government

The re-establishment of some kind of self-government in Northern Ireland is the kind of solution on which agreement is most likely to be reached between the two communities in Northern Ireland. It is the solution that would go closest to meeting the aspirations of each, since both communities are now seeking some form of self-determination.

There can, of course, be no question of setting up again a Stormont Parliament or Government on the old basis. No British Government would risk it and even if it would, the Northern minority would never consent. But a mini-Westminster is not the only possible form of democratic institution. It is possible to construct a system that would give Northern Ireland at least as great a degree of self-determination as it previously had, while making a return to the old sectarian-type government impossible. Use of proportional representation would work against extreme polarisation on sectarian lines. One of PR's alleged defects in the Republic—that it has excessively blurred political distinctions—would even be a virtue in Northern conditions.

Again, the Westminster practice that 51 per cent of votes in the Parliament or Assembly elects the government is not sacred. If in a new Northern Assembly elected by proportional representation a government had to have the affirmative votes of at least 75 per cent of the members in order to take office, then no government in Northern Ireland could come to power on a purely sectarian base, although of course it must be recognised that this would make it more difficult to form a cohesive administration, particularly in view of the large number of different groups likely to be represented in a Northern Assembly, at least in the early years.

These safeguards could be reinforced by some form of fundamental law or Bill of Rights aimed specifically at eliminating or preventing sectarian practices and backed up by a guaranteed right of appeal for every citizen to judicial or other bodies wholly independent of the Northern Ireland government. That machinery, which might cover matters such as the drawing of electoral boundaries, public appointments, or any action of government where there was prima facie evidence of sectarianism, could be operated jointly by the British and Irish Governments.

Proportional Representation

The present electoral system in Northern Ireland forces people to choose between candidates on a basis of purely sectarian loyalty; to avoid splitting the tribal vote people feel they cannot risk supporting candidates not clearly identified as champions of their own faction. In the present political climate of Northern Ireland, this system must inevitably elect a disproportionately large number of extremists on one side or the other.

The multi-seat transferable vote system would have several important effects. First, it would make it possible for a much wider range of candidates to offer themselves without the danger of vote-splitting. Secondly, moderate voters in either community, having voted first for the candidates of the party they support, would in many cases pass their later preferences to candidates of moderate parties associated with the other community rather than to extremists of their own religious persuasion. Thirdly, even parties which are not identified as moderate may feel it desirable to select and put forward at least some candidates acceptable to moderates, in the hope of attracting their later preferences.

In a five or seven-seat constituency incorporating a typical cross-section of the Northern Ireland population, the main contenders in an election will include the Unionist Party, Republicans (of either or both wings), the Alliance Party, the SDLP, Northern Ireland Labour, the Democratic Unionists and perhaps Vanguard. In that contest no party could hope to take more than one or two seats in the constituency on a purely sectarian appeal. To benefit from transfers of votes on the elimination of the weaker contenders, the major parties would have to balance their candidate's slate to get as wide a spread as possible.

These calculations depend, of course, on the assumption that a majority of people will in fact use the transferable vote. It is arguable that feelings in Northern Ireland between Protestant and Catholic might be so bitter that even later preferences would not be given across sectarian lines. Such evidence as there is, however, does not support this view. The success of the Alliance Party in bringing Protestants and Catholics together in the same organisation and in generating considerable support in many districts gives hope that many people would use their later preferences if only to ensure the defeat of those candidates whom they most disliked.

In the present fluid state of Northern Ireland politics the multi-seat transferable vote system would give at least six parties representation in any new Northern Ireland assembly. At least three of these (Alliance, Northern Ireland Labour and SDLP) will each include both Catholics and Protestants in their membership and almost certainly in their representation in the assembly, particularly if this assembly is substantially larger than the old Stormont, as it is generally agreed should be the case. Between them these three parties might even conceivably control 50 per cent or more of the total seats, and even if their support were a good deal lower than this they could certainly be a dominant element in any government which required for its support 75 per cent of the membership of the Parliament.

75 per cent Majority Principle

Because of fifty years of bad experience at Stormont it is obviously essential that real safeguards against a reversion to the old Stormont be built into any new constitution. But in building in those safeguards it is important to avoid saddling it with arrangements which would effectively paralyse any new system or which would wish on the people of Northern Ireland structures that it might subsequently be difficult to get rid of and which might prove cumbersome or inappropriate. Past history in other countries frequently shows that cleverly devised constitutions which are intellectually neat, can work out disastrously in practice. I have suggested the 75 per cent support proviso with some reserve because, while it would obviously ensure that a clearly sectarian government could not achieve power, it would also obviously create a danger of stalemate. Nevertheless, I believe some provision of this kind is necessary to ensure that the authority of such a government is accepted by both communities.

There is an obvious reluctance, particularly in Britain, to consider delegating to any new Northern government powers as extensive as those formerly exercised by Stormont. I think this view is mistaken. Most Northern Ireland people want self-government. It would be a mistake to stop short at an emasculated form of this because of past experience. The right lesson to draw from the past is not that Northern Ireland cannot be trusted with self-government, it is that the peculiar problems of Northern Ireland require special structures and safeguards to make self-government work effectively—such as this 75 per cent majority provision.

In so far as this implies that both religious groups must be represented as such in the government the concept of 'community' government has been put forward. This seems to assume that Northern Ireland will continue to be permanently polarised very largely into Catholic and Protestant groups. Community government would have the merit of guaranteeing participation in government to each community in proportion to its strength, but it would have serious disadvantages. It would tend to build into the system, and therefore perpetuate, this polarisation. It would tend to inhibit the interplay of normal political forces in the community, since the road to power would run through two clearly defined sectarian channels rather than through normal party politics. Non-sectarian parties such as the Alliance would find it difficult to remain relevant.

Participation for the minority can be far more healthily provided for by safeguards that would prevent the re-emergence of a purely sectarian regime without preventing normal political activity. A solution might be found by providing that all political groups must be represented in government proportionately to their numbers but this could inhibit effective leadership and the making of self-defined political choices—which is what government is about. The 75 per cent majority requirement could assure the representation of a wide range of groups in government while avoiding the excessive rigidity of proportional government.

As for the need to make provision for an eventual return to a normal majority rule system, the 75 per cent positive vote requirement could be introduced for a limited term—say five years—after which it would either lapse automatically, or have to be renewed by Act of the British Parliament. Alternatively, there could be provision for a constitutional referendum to amend provisions of this sort as the Northern Ireland community evolved towards more normal politics and as such changes became possible and generally acceptable.

The Bill of Rights

Already implied in the foregoing is what would amount to a written constitution for Northern Ireland. This concept should be taken further by introducing as part of the new constitution a basic law guaranteeing civil rights. Under this law all forms of discrimination based on race or religion by any public authority or public servant would be illegal. But, clearly, given the present reality in Northern Ireland, to make such a law convincing, it would have to be beyond the power of the Northern Ireland Government to alter it and the ultimate level of appeal for cases arising under it would have to be an objective court outside Northern Ireland. This need could be met by establishing a Court of Human Rights, with perhaps judges drawn equally from Britain and the Republic, and a President supplied alternatively by each.

A convincing legal remedy of this kind for cases involving any form of discrimination would go a long way towards limiting the duration of a system of safeguards against sectarianism in the political system itself, since, even if a 'Protestant' or 'Catholic' government took power, the basic law and the Human Rights Court would effectively prevent it from passing laws or taking executive action of a sectarian kind.

A Council of Ireland?

A self-governing Northern Ireland could not of course exist in a vacuum. Its very existence would be owed to the close co-operation of the British and Irish Governments formalised by treaty. While the constitutional and economic links with Britain would be maintained, there would have to be a much closer link also with the Republic.

Some form of the Council of Ireland concept is known to be acceptable to a large section of Northern Protestant opinion and was indeed proposed by the Unionist Government shortly before it was removed. What form might this Council take? What would be its powers and how should they be defined?

Here there may be lessons to be drawn from the structure of the EEC. A treaty of which the Republic, Northern Ireland and Britain would all be signatories would define those areas of responsibility coming under the Council of Ireland. The most obvious such field would be economic development. The Council's responsibility could include control of such matters as industrial development, tourism, agriculture and fisheries and regional policy for the whole country. It could also have a role in administering funds provided by Britain to promote economic development in Northern Ireland. The Council itself could include ministers from the Northern and Southern Governments. There could also be an authority headed by an independent commission selected from North and South which would carry out decisions taken under the treaty and propose policy to the council. And there could be added an assembly of parliamentarians from North and South with an advisory role.

Internal security would be another possible field for some form of common action. There might, for example, be an extension of extradition to cover all offences, political or otherwise, committed on either side of the border. A security committee to cover the whole island might be established under the Council.

Such a Council could be established on the understanding that its powers could be extended with the consent of both Governments. That would leave open the possibility of progress towards closer formal unity while giving either government a veto over any such steps. It may be argued that the existence of such a veto would in effect ensure that Northern Ireland would not agree to any such extension of the power of the common institutions. That would be likely to happen only if the concept were not proving successful and if Northern Ireland remained suspicious of closer involvement with the South. In that case, closer unity would not be desirable anyway. But in my view the effect would be different. It would put continuous pressure on those, particularly in the Republic, who desire closer unity, to ensure that nothing was done there to alienate Northern opinion—that on the contrary, a continuing effort was made to create in the Republic the kind of society with which Northerners would want closer association.

This formula would give formal unity in practical fields where it would be of real value. At the same time, it would guarantee the Northern majority against absorption into the Republic against their will. Its basic virtue would be that it would provide for real progress towards national unity, but in realistic stages which could be adjusted to prevailing circumstances and to the wishes of the people on both sides of the border. It would avoid the unrealistic and oversimplified approach of Yes or No to union with the Republic on an 'all or nothing' basis. Meaningful unity is not, as the traditional anti-partitionists implied, a simple matter of rubbing out a line on the map. It is a matter of the two parts of the country growing gradually together, a process which would have to be preceded by a growing together of the two communities in Northern Ireland.

It will, of course, be the task of a peace conference to negotiate the details of such arrangements. But it might also be worth following EEC precedent to the extent of writing into the treaty a timetable for certain agreed extensions of the Council's powers—an extension which would, however, be subject to blocking by one or other government, or by referendum in either part of the country if called by either government. In other words, certain steps towards greater unity such as adding to the powers of the parliamentary assembly, or electing the assembly by direct vote on a thirty-two county basis, could come into effect automatically unless blocked.

Meanwhile what would happen to 'the British link'? Clearly economic relations between Britain and Ireland would have to remain extremely close. Any such scheme as that outlined would not be practical without substantial subventions from Britain to maintain standards in Northern Ireland at their present level. In addition, Northerners are unlikely to agree, at least in the short-term, to give up their representation at Westminster, even in a climate of much warmer co-operation between North and South. But the Council of Ireland treaty could provide for some changing of the former political links at an agreed future time.

At the same time a joint British/Irish ministerial and/or parliamentary council might be established which would handle matters of common interest between Britain and Ireland. The concept of interchangeable citizenship might also be explored—e.g. that all citizens of Ireland and Britain would enjoy full citizen's rights in each other's countries—the right to vote, the right to participate in politics, the right to serve in the public service without discrimination, the right to protection abroad.

Fine Gael Front Bench
Northern Ireland policy statement[1]

Michael Sweetman

Fine Gael has been giving careful and continuous consideration to the situation in the Six Counties and the Front Bench considers that certain steps should be taken immediately to deal with this situation.

The present troubles in Northern Ireland find their origins in fear: fear of each other by both sections of the Community.

A small dominant group in Northern Ireland, having secured power by the division of the country, and having continued within that area to operate a thinly-disguised continuation of the Ascendancy of earlier times, fears the loss of its power and its privileged position.

Moreover, by playing on the fears of ordinary people, who for generations have been the victims of suitable propaganda, this dominant group has succeeded in creating and maintaining amongst the ordinary Protestant people a fear of unfair treatment, not alone within an independent Irish State, should the division of the country be ended, but even within Northern Ireland itself, should equal rights to employment and housing be extended to all sections of the community.

In this way the ruling group has succeeded in securing for half a century popular support amongst a majority of the Protestant population for the maintenance of its regime of privilege. It has been aided in this by the irresponsible lack of concern of successive British governments at the exploitation of the minority in Northern Ireland. This situation has not been helped by repeated threats against Northern Ireland from subversive elements in the Republic, which has lent colour to the propaganda campaign of the extreme elements of the Unionist Party, or by unwise and inconsistent policies in this part of the country.

[1] Statement issued 1969

Three conflicting policies have been simultaneously pursued here:

1) Vainly trying to generate international pressure to force Britain to 'hand over' the North.

2) Seeking through closer and better relations with Britain to persuade that country to move towards a solution of the Northern Ireland problem in conjunction with the Republic.

3) Improving relations with the Northern Ireland Government with a view to reducing the tensions which perpetuate the division of Ireland.

The first of these has been used mainly for domestic political purposes in the Republic, but by its use has rendered ineffective the other two policies.

The dominant group in Northern Ireland, aided by British lack of interest, plotting by subversive elements in the Republic, and the pursuit of conflicting policies here, has succeeded in keeping alive the unreasoning fears of many members of the Protestant majority in that area. As a result, even a non-sectarian movement for civil rights, the achievement of whose objectives would benefit the Protestant working population as well as the Catholic, is seen by many Protestants as a threat to their way of life—a threat which extremists resist by violence.

At the same time, the Catholic minority, many of them confined to ghettoes in the cities and towns by the operation of a discriminatory housing policy, lives in fear of attack by Protestant extremists, its memories of past attacks being revived in every generation by fresh outbursts, as in 1920/22, 1935 and now 1969.

This problem of mutual fear is the real problem and until it is resolved the people of the North will never be able to live normal lives, whether they find themselves continuing in Northern Ireland, or in a united Ireland.

Within Northern Ireland itself there has been a growing recognition of this, especially amongst the Catholic minority, and as a result, the emphasis in political life amongst the minority has changed during the past decade from traditional anti-partitionism to winning civil rights for all sections of the community.

The aim is in the first instance to create a normal political situation free from sectarian distortions and from the gerrymandering power of the dominant group working skillfully to maintain power and privilege. The achievement of this aim would lay the foundations for the ending of the present national division.

It is the duty of political parties in the Republic, who must be concerned for the people of Northern Ireland, and especially for the exploited and maltreated minority, to recognise these facts and to have regard to the wishes of this Northern minority. This duty is reinforced by the self-evident fact that, force as a weapon of policy having been rejected by all responsible political groups in the Republic, the only way in which the present divided state of this island can, or should be modified is with the consent of a majority of the people of Northern Ireland.

Accordingly, the following course of action is proposed with a view to helping to create peace and reconciliation in Northern Ireland, and with a view to hastening the reunion of Ireland with the goodwill of people on both sides of the Border:

1) The development in the Republic of policy with regard to Northern Ireland should be carried out in consultation with those democratically elected representatives in Northern Ireland who are opposed to policies of privilege and sectarianism.

2) The Government here should concentrate its diplomatic efforts on securing maximum British support for the creation of normal democracy and a just society in Northern Ireland, and for initiating greater cooperation between the three governments.

3) Towards these ends, the Government should press the British Government to reconstitute the RUC as a civil unarmed police force, similar to the Garda Síochána, recruited from all groups in the community, and confined to normal police duties. It should also support the disbandment of the B Specials and press for the maintenance of order by a generally neutral force.

4) The Government should press, not alone for the immediate implementation of the one-man one-vote principle in local elections, but also for the creation of electoral areas with boundaries fairly and impartially drawn, and for guarantees that gerrymandering will not be possible in future in Northern Ireland.

5) The Government should, after appropriate consultation with Northern opinion, press the British Government to ensure representation of the minority in the Northern Ireland Government as the sole means of reassuring the minority as to the full and continued implementation of the proposed reforms, and fair treatment for this minority.

6) The Government should initiate discussions with the British and Northern Ireland Governments for the creation of a body similar to the Council of Ireland envisaged at the time of the Treaty.

7) The Government, and the political parties in Dáil Éireann, should assert formally their rejection of force as a solution to the division of Ireland, and should clearly state their intention to work towards a voluntary reunion of the people of both parts of Ireland.

8) The Government and the political parties in Dáil Éireann should, in consultation with representatives of all sections of the community in Northern Ireland, initiate a study of the changes necessary in the Constitution and laws of the Republic in order to make them acceptable to the widest possible spectrum of opinion in Ireland.

9) The political parties in the Republic should pledge themselves to work together to create in the Republic conditions of economic prosperity and social justice, including social welfare arrangements comparable with those in Northern Ireland, so as to eliminate any economic or social obstacles to the reunification of the country.

10) The Government should immediately establish an all-party committee for Northern Ireland affairs to secure the implementation of the above policies.

The case for some sort of a united Ireland rests essentially on this: that the Northern Ireland minority will not accept permanent full integration of Northern Ireland into the United Kingdom as a final solution. But the Northern majority also want self-government, and a wholly independent Northern Ireland, even if acceptable to both communities in the North, is impracticable politically and economically. The only possible compromise between the aspirations of the Northern majority and Northern minority is one that includes a close relationship ·with the rest of the island, combined with maintenance of the distinctiveness of the Northern community and full recognition of the British part of this country's heritage.

Now that membership of the European Community is bringing us into a more balanced relationship with Britain, we can more easily afford to recognise the British strand in our heritage without fearing any compromise of our national integrity. We should by now have gained sufficient self-confidence to put aside the extreme attitudes of past conflicts.

History cannot be used to justify a united Ireland. History does not confer 'rights' of the kind implied in traditional nationalist ideology. A more modem concept is of the basic rights of the individual. It is the living who have rights to organise their affairs in whatever way suits them best. We do not owe any debt to history to fulfil supposed objectives of the past. History does not confer any rights to take away the basic rights of others to choose how they will live. Nor can the concept of democracy be stretched to justify a nationalistic claim to impose unity; even if democratic principles were violated fifty years ago in dividing Ireland, the wrongs of the past do not invalidate the basic rights of the individual today. In this sense, the citizen of Northern Ireland has the right today freely to choose his own future within the Northern Ireland framework, even though the establishment of that framework fifty years ago may have been a wrong or even an unjust decision.

Agreement in principle on the restoration of self-government in Northern Ireland seems a realistic possibility at any conference including the main constitutional parties in Northern Ireland—Unionist, Nationalist, SDLP, Alliance, Northern Ireland Labour, Liberal. It would go a long way to moderating the resentment at the removal of Stormont felt by a large section of moderate Protestant opinion. It could—indeed must—guarantee full equality of status and opportunity to Northern Catholics. It would not, of course, satisfy the more extreme 'Republicans' or the small group of Protestants who genuinely want complete integration into the United Kingdom. But at least as an interim solution it would satisfy the vast majority of people in Northern Ireland.

In the longer term a united Ireland will come about as Protestants as well as Catholics in Northern Ireland as in the Republic come to believe that a political link between the two areas is in their best interest. And that belief will come, not from the kind of pressure or coercion implicit in the ill-considered approach to national unity adopted in the Republic over a period of fifty years, but from the discovery by all concerned that it is possible for us to live and work together in peace, and that in so doing we can create an Ireland capable of satisfying the aspirations of all our people.

Education policy[1]

Michael Sweetman

Education is at the very core of our present national problem. Our system of education, and popular attitudes towards it, exemplify the reasons why Ireland remains in 1971 as divided as ever despite fifty years of independence in this part of the country. Our traditional system of education gives a position to the Catholic Church which, while it has been accepted without question by the vast majority of people in the South, would not be acceptable to a majority of people in Northern Ireland in any 32-county state. At least some people are now thinking again seriously about possible ways in which, over a period of time, the present Northern tragedy might be permanently revolved on some kind of all-Ireland basis acceptable to a majority both North and South. It is in this context that I want to examine what issues we in the South have to face in the field of education and the direction in which we will have to move if we are in earnest about a 32-county Irish society.

In doing this I want to make one thing clear. I am not attacking the past role of the Church in Irish education. It is beyond dispute that priests and nuns have for generations carried a large share of the burden of Irish education with steadfast idealism. Their commitment has in fact permitted the state to avoid its obligation to provide a just and comprehensive educational system available to all. Instead it has shamelessly exploited the willingness of the Church to provide education at very low cost. However, painful though it may be, the fact has to be faced that part of the price of national unity would be major changes in these arrangements.

I would like to dispose first of one common misconception—the notion that it is possible to contrive some form of 'neutral' education which does not influence children's religious or philosophical think-

1 Paper delivered to the Humanist Conference on *Catholic education and democracy* in Malahide 1971

ing and leaves them free 'to make up their own minds' when they reach maturity. There is no such thing as 'neutral' education. Any living educational system must pass on from one generation to another the traditions, values and attitudes of the society in which it works. One of the most fundamental responsibilities of both parents and educators is to guide the development of children in the light of a philosophical framework and value system in which they themselves believe. To refuse this guidance is to evade one of our most solemn obligations to our children.

An educational system, then, cannot be philosophically or morally neutral. Yet, in a mixed society like Ireland, where religious and philosophical attitudes differ, the problem is to find a just balance. There are those who do not accept religion at all and others (the vast majority) who claim to be Christians but disagree about what that means. How can these different viewpoints be accommodated within the same educational system? The traditional answer in Ireland has been that they can. It is argued that, to begin with, education is really no business of the state's but a private matter and that each group should therefore provide its own. By implication, that concept accepted social inequality in education, because under it the education a child received depended on parents' ability to pay, or, the extent to which religious or others were prepared to educate selected children free, on conditions determined by the educators, not the parents.

It is now widely recognised that the community, acting through the state, has a responsibility to ensure equality of educational opportunity for everybody, irrespective of their social status or means. The state can only do that by itself providing education. That is why education in Ireland is now the subject of increasing controversy—we are in the middle of a conflict between two apparently incompatible propositions, the belief in private responsibility for education with its inevitable inequalities, and the belief in equality of educational opportunity with the inevitable state responsibility.

How can this be resolved? Firstly, it must be said that the shared values, beliefs and traditions of Irish people cover a vastly greater spectrum than those on which they differ. Until a few years ago it was the custom for both Catholics and Protestants to stress the extent to which they differed. In recent years this has been dramatically reversed. It has been reversed precisely because more and more people of common sense felt that these differences, while of extreme importance to theologians and church rulers, seemed to have little practical relevance in the world in which they had to live. What seemed important to the ordinary Christian was the basic corpus of belief and values which all Christians shared. That is why we have today a degree of ecumenism which would have quite deeply shocked Irish churchmen even twenty years ago when I myself was at school and the need to uphold the unique truth of one's own brand of Christianity and expose the falseness of all others was taken for granted for 'Catholic' education, if not quite so explicitly for Protestant.

A lot has changed since then. A great blast of common sense has blown away many of the cobwebs. For the Christian churches the question now is not what kind of Christians are people going to be, but whether they are going to be Christians at all. But we must recognise that in Ireland at least, whether people profess to be Christians or not, they continue to share with Christians a great deal of common value and attitude, at least in regard to how one should live and conduct society. There is enough practical agreement between everybody who lives in Ireland to make it possible for people of different religious or philosophical views to share a common curriculum for virtually all subjects and to follow it in the same school. This is already happening in the vocational schools, and to a limited extent in some other secondary schools which have broken free from strict sectarianism.

Great stress has been laid in the past, particularly by the Catholic Church in Ireland, on the critical importance of explicitly 'Catholic' schools. It was held that only in such a fully 'Catholic atmosphere' could the faith and loyalty of Catholic children by fully developed and secured. In the last few years many Irish Catholic parents have come to question this proposition.

For one thing, the assumption that education can be isolated in this way from the world around looks more and more unreal. Besides, it is less and less clear precisely what it is that needs to be specially protected in this way. Many Catholic priests today, as well as Catholic parents, take the view that children are going to have to live in a world in which they will meet all kinds of different views and attitudes and that far from trying to isolate them from this they should learn from as early an age as possible how to live with it. There is plenty of evidence from our experience in this country that young people who have gone through this enclosed form of education find themselves completely disorientated when they go into the world, particularly when they emigrate and are tempted to reject in total a value system which they cannot make relevant, while at the same time not being equipped to construct for themselves an alternative. There is plenty of evidence that, whatever its justification, 'Catholic' education in Ireland is not particularly effective in keeping people within the faith, once they move outside the sheltered and, in terms of the modern world, somewhat artificial atmosphere of this country.

Let us be blunt about it. What this is really about is institutional power in the community. There was a time when, because education was scarce, those who supplied it had a vital instrument of power in their hands. All religious denominations recognised this and have fought to keep that power. In Northern Ireland the position of the Catholic Church in the matter is understandable. In a minority group which feels itself under constant threat from a majority, any bit of power which it holds to help keep its head above water is jealously defended. Yet despite this, the strict sectarian division of education in Northern Ireland has surely not been a good thing. It has contributed immeasurably to the climate of hostility and mutual incomprehension between the two communities. If religious bigotry is to be rooted out in Northern Ireland, a key place to start is to bring together young people of the different religions at their most impressionable age. It is significant that the Rose Report showed a two to one majority in 1968 among Northern Catholics in favour of integrated education. Despite the obvious difficulties in moving towards that at this particular moment, the Catholic community in Northern Ireland should take a decision in principle in favour of integrated education.

The situation in the South is, of course, different. Here, with a 95 per cent Catholic population the vast majority of school children are Catholics. Until recently most Catholic parents accepted as a matter of course the right of the Church to full control of these children's education. The religious minority were concerned to preserve their identity by keeping going their own system of sectarian schools. But the kind of clerical control of education which we have in Ireland is not defended simply so that children can be taught religion.

There is in fact plenty of evidence that children's religious or philosophical attitudes are almost entirely determined by their home environment and only very marginally by school. Rather it is claimed that Catholic education by maintaining a complete 'Catholic atmosphere', permeates the child's personality and through him the whole community, with denominational religion.

This is an increasingly unattractive concept even to many loyal Catholics. There is, however, little evidence that even if such permeation is the desired result of a 'Catholic atmosphere' in the schools, it is effective. Irish society has become increasingly secularised in parallel with the outside world.

We have, then, north and south of the border, a system of sectarian education which has developed over the years for perhaps quite valid historic reasons.

We now face the need for fundamental change in this system, not only for reasons of national unity but because even within this state new demands are being made on the government. The solution now being proposed seems to me to be going precisely in the opposite direction to what is desirable. So far from moving towards a uniform system under which all children in the community will go to school together and thereby learn to live together irrespective of religion, it is proposed to formalise the sectarian division of religion—to build it rigidly into our political institutions in a way in which it has never been built in before. It is bad enough to have a sectarian system which exists simply because it has evolved—it would be infinitely worse to make such a system permanent and official. Our task in Ireland today is to get people out of the religious ghettos into which history has put them, not herd them in tighter and close the exits.

The right concept certainly is a community school. But that should mean a school open to and acceptable to all the children of the community. It should include all the local community's educational activities. It should be under the democratic control of the local community. Its curriculum and atmosphere should be based on what is common to all members of the community and it should avoid offence to the susceptibilities of particular groups within that community. At the same time, each group should have full facilities for their own religious instruction or for other specialised needs of this kind. In other words, a community school should be a miniature model of the kind of society we want. It should be designed to train people to live together in harmony and mutual respect. If, by a divided educational system, we teach people divisiveness, we can hardly be surprised if they find it difficult to live together when they grow up.

Having stated that ideal one must accept that at this moment the churches have a dominant role in Irish education. There is no question of abruptly taking away this role—most Irish people would not want that. Dedicated clergy have an enormous contribution to make to any system of Irish education. But to accept this is not to concede that as parents and as citizens we can or should hand over to any hierarchy or private organisation within the state that ultimate responsibility for the education of our children which belongs to us alone. Large numbers of loyal Catholics and Protestants want their churches to continue a very active role in the education of their children, but at the same time believe that it is to parents that God has given the responsibility and parents who must discharge it. For this reason, control of the community school in each area must rest with them. What we need is a school board system under which a majority of members are elected by proportional representation, while an additional number are co-opted to represent special interests, or nominated by religious or other groups where this is appropriate.

It would be wrong to think in terms of rapidly introducing a standardised community school system throughout the country. Each area has its own peculiar needs. Each area has its own existing situation. What is called for is evolution, not revolution. Those now doing the job and who have such an enormous contribution to make must be able to continue making that contribution. An arrangement which would suit one area might not suit another. But surely we have in fact begun the wrong way around. There has been a bureaucratic effort to impose a uniform system on the whole country. We should begin the other way around and first establish our school boards. These would then have the responsibility of identifying the particular needs of their own area, and planning to meet them in the light of the particular situation as it now exists, and obviously in full cooperation with existing schools.

The community school should not only be non-denominational; it should also be designed to eliminate class distinctions in education. Within our present educational structure there are strong class connotations attaching to the different educational streams. These class distinctions can have no place in a socially just Irish society. If we are

[195]

serious about eliminating social inequality in later life, the right place to begin is at school.

A community school should be much more than just a school in the old-fashioned sense. It should become the cultural heart of each local community, catering as much for its adult members as for the young. It is a well-worn cliché that in modern society education cannot end with school, yet we have done little in practical terms to recognise that. Ideally, a community school would have attached to it, not only teachers in the present sense but staff who had other responsibilities for organising and leading community activity.

To summarise then, a united Ireland means a new kind of educational system—not some flabby, neutral thing based on a vague liberalism, but a system fully recognising that strong beliefs and convictions are good things, but that in a healthy Irish society there will be a diversity of such belief and conviction and that that too is good. Our education must impart certain basic values common to our society, while teaching us how to disagree on many things, while living and working together in peace and brotherhood.

That kind of educational system can only exist if it is firmly grounded in local democracy. If the people of each locality are given the responsibility and the means, I am confident that the just rights of minority groups will not be taken away and here I am speaking of the whole of Ireland, not just of the 26 Counties. That has been proved in the vocational school system here already and in many other specific fields in which ordinary people of common sense have been allowed to get on with the constructive work of running their own community. Education is too serious a matter to be left to anybody else.

The time has come for us to start facing up honestly to the real implications of national unity, in education no less than in other fields. These implications may be extremely distasteful to many and those who point them out will be correspondingly unpopular. Yet if a united Ireland means anything as an ideal, it is the ideal of the pluralist society. Pluralism in Ireland can only work if the source of power is the individual citizen and his vote equal in all respects. It can only work if this principle of equality is raised to the status of an absolute in our political and social life. That is why one of the first moves towards such a society, and therefore towards national unity, must be an educational system under full local democratic control and guaranteeing to every child absolute equality of educational opportunity. What we do in our schools today will be the pattern for the whole of our society tomorrow. The current tragic situation in our country is also an exciting opportunity: let us grasp it courageously with both hands. We may not have it again.

After Stormont[1]

Michael Sweetman

The suspension of Stormont offers Ireland an exciting opportunity to correct some of the mistakes of the past and to make a new start.

It means a major injustice removed. It is not a permanent solution but it provides the opportunity to work one out. To do that requires a period of peace. It is perfectly obvious that what the vast majority of people in Northern Ireland of both communities want is peace.

We in the Republic must make up our minds to the fact that the permanent solution is going to be a compromise. Few people in the South yet adequately realise what such a compromise implies. After fifty years of anti-partitionist propaganda, most people still instinctively think of the taking over of Northern Ireland by the South and the imposition on it of the South's political and cultural values.

Most people in Northern Ireland want self-government. That includes most supporters of the Unionist Party, most of the Nationalists, the Alliance Party and of course the Rev. Ian Paisley (despite his tongue-in-cheek call for complete integration into the United Kingdom). There is not now, and is unlikely to be in the future, a major political grouping in Northern Ireland campaigning for complete integration into the UK. Yet recent events have ensured one thing—Northern Ireland cannot have self-government either in the old form or on a purely six county basis. No British administration is going to take the risk of re-establishing self-government in Northern Ireland without the wholehearted consent of the vast majority of people in both religious communities. That will only be got by a compromise under which Northern Ireland will develop close links with the rest of the country, while retaining either in its own right or through a new relationship between the whole of Ireland and Britain close ties with the United Kingdom.

1 *Sunday Press* April 1972

Our responsibility now in the South is to help Northern Ireland achieve self-government again as quickly as possible. We must do that without pushing for any prior commitment to national unity (too often our interest in Northern Ireland affairs has seemed to Northern Protestants no more than fishing in troubled waters for our own advantage). We must accept that only a self-governing Northern Ireland can discuss with us the long-term future of the whole country. We ourselves meanwhile must evolve a new philosophy of compromise and pluralism.

That means in many ways gong back to an older concept of Irish patriotism. Wolfe Tone's name is regularly evoked in support of 20th-century sectarian nationalism. We need to go back to the 18th-century and honestly examine what he really stood for. It had little in common with most of what is now said and done in his name.

By suspending Stormont the British Government has swept away a great deal of what was done in Northern Ireland since 1912. We too have got to go back to 1912 and relinquish a great deal of what has happened since in the South in order that both parts of the country can make a new start. We would have to admit frankly that the sectarian nationalism which has dominated the South since then was in many ways a response to the Orange Unionism of the North.

How difficult this is going to be is exemplified in Proinsias Mac-Aonghusa's article in last week's *Sunday Press*. He dismisses the Northern Ireland Alliance Party on the grounds that ordinary Irishmen are not decent, reasonable people like members of the Alliance but are condemned by their nature to political extremism. He suggests that people like the Alliance who are preaching a policy of compromise— of working together across sectarian boundaries to create a new society by peaceful means—are 'drawingroom characters', 'castle Catholics and castle Protestants', 'milk and water people'. Greatest sin of all, they are 'nice middle-class people'. Therefore they cannot 'represent anything real'.

Here are a number of preconceptions or prejudices which will have to go if we are to have any chance of an All-Ireland community at some time in the future. Firstly, the assumption that extremism and intolerance are the yardsticks for validity or reality in politics. Political extremism is not necessarily better or higher than toleration, moderation or common sense. Nor do the vast majority of Irish people of any class necessarily think it is. We have seen in the last few days the efforts of the women of Andersonstown supported by the vast majority of people all over Ireland to persuade Seán MacStiofáin alias John Stephenson to give them the chance of peace. Mr MacAonghusa sneers at the Alliance Party as being the kind of Irish political party that the English love. But what could be more 'typically Irish' in the traditional English sense than the spectacle of an Englishman thinly disguised as an Irishman ensconced in a comfortable and safe haven in the Republic inciting the Irish of the North to murder each other to satisfy his political fanaticism.

We must be on our guard too against efforts, conscious or otherwise, to replace the old sectarian bigotry based on religion with a new one based on 'class'. The orderliness and commonsense of the Alliance Conference which Mr MacAonghusa contemptuously dismisses as 'middle-class' and therefore not real, in fact reflects basic qualities of the Ulsterman of any class. To put it very bluntly, in the new Ireland we are going to have to accept as perfectly valid qualities which, in the Catholic present culture of the South, were dismissed as 'Protestant' or 'Ascendancy', or 'middle-class' or 'British'. Despite the high-flown language of Party manifestos 'Republicanism' whether of the Official, Provisional, Aontacht Éireann or Fianna Fáil variety, has a strong flavour of Catholic Nationalism. Despite lip-service to pluralism and tolerance, each of these groups have consistently sought to impose on all Irishmen a narrow concept of Irishness involving the primacy of Gaelic culture, the rejection of the British strands in our tradition, a particular view of history which painted Irishmen who fought against Britain as automatically goodies and those who believed in British rule as automatically baddies, and finally, an uneasy tolerance rather than open-hearted acceptance of Protestants and Protestant values. It is not from that kind of Republicanism, with its glorification of violence in the past and its incitement to violence in the present, that the new Ireland will come. Rather it will come from those despised moderates who are also the vast majority of people on this island who want to find ways of living in peace together and working constructively for a better future in real and practical ways. This is their chance.

What practical steps should we take to this end? Firstly, as I have said, we must co-operate fully and in the spirit of genuine friendship in the re-establishment of self-government in Northern Ireland without seeking to impose our own wishes on the people of that part of the country. That having been done we can move to practical unity in a number of important ways. Here we might find a useful model in some of the institutions of the EEC. An obvious field for all-Ireland co-operation would be in trade and economic development. A treaty between Dublin, a self-governing Northern Ireland and Britain could establish an All-Ireland Economic Community with a structure similar to that of the EEC, i.e. a Commission with responsibilities for formulating policy and executing it and a Council of Ministers representing the governments of both parts of the country to take decisions. The powers and scope of these institutions would be precisely defined by treaty as those of the EEC are by the Treaty of Rome.

Another obvious field for co-operation is that of internal security. Again, joint institutions operating under a treaty could work to preserve the security of the whole island. Education and social security are other fields in which common action might be taken.

The great strength of this approach to unity is its practical step by step nature. It can go as quickly or as slowly as the parties want it to go. It can cover as wide a range as the parties think it valuable to cover, but does not involve the parties in commitments which are not clearly defined and agreed. Its success would depend, not on the triumph of one part of the country over the other, but on the willingness to work together—to find common solutions to common problems, to find compromises between conflicting interests.

In a sense, we in the South are now entering on a period of probation, during which we have an opportunity to demonstrate that we are in fact mature enough to participate in an All-Ireland system based on genuine mutual respect and equality. We will have to think a lot deeper than fiddling about with paper changes in our Constitution or the more blatantly sectarian of our laws. Many of the values and assumptions of Northern society are different to the value system which in the last fifty years has become official orthodoxy in the South. It is not just a question of religion or of race. An important ingredient is the much stronger urban traditions of the North compared with the predominantly rural background in the South. And for us in the South it will involve accepting close ties with the other island—not in our present mealy-mouthed, shame-faced way, but frankly, as part of the culture, tradition and more than a thousand years of common history which we share.

All the peoples of Western Europe are turning away from the quarrels which divided them so bitterly in the past towards a new emphasis on that which they have in common, stressing where their interests coincide and they can work together for mutual benefit rather than the points at which they conflict. This is the time for us in our own island to set about doing the same.

The important thing at present is to keep a clear view of longer-term considerations and avoid being panicked by the pressure of events into damaging short-term moves. For example, the Government must resist the temptation to try for a short-cut out of certain of its difficulties by resorting to internment. There is a fundamental danger for any State in meeting lawlessness with lawlessness. Certain people have openly declared that their purpose is to destroy this State by violence. The overwhelming majority of people in this State have repeatedly made clear in election after election and through all the organs of public opinion and public information that they do not support this. The soundest way of retaining the support of this vast majority is by holding firmly to the just application of democratically created laws. If under pressure the normal lawful processes of the State are suspended, then those who are seeking at this moment to destroy those processes will have achieved a very large part of their purpose.

It is important to make sure that our refusal to resort to internment in this part of the country is not interpreted in any way as support for terrorism in the North, or an unwillingness to apply the full rigour of the law to illegal organisations or unlawful acts here. In this whole situation there is a fundamental division between those who believe they have the right to use force on their fellow-citizens to impose political ideas which those citizens do not share, and on the other side the vast majority of people, North and South, who believe in peaceful and democratic solution of political problems. The Government here must make it unambiguously clear, and continue to make it clear, not only by its words but by its actions, on which side it belongs.

It must be obvious to those who take a longer-term view that the situation in the North can only be resolved by agreement, unless one accepts as an alternative a bloody struggle between the two communities in which one finally defeats and virtually annihilates the other. That possibility must be so abhorrent to the vast majority of decent people that the search for an agreement must be intensified in order to avoid the other outcome. Such an agreement must involve in the first instance acceptance by the two communities in Northern Ireland of equal citizenship for all. That will imply on the side of the Northern majority accepting the need to build a radically new political and social structure in Northern Ireland to ensure not only that no new inequality between the two communities will be created in future, but that the accumulated inequality of fifty years of injustice will be eliminated as quickly as possible. The legacy of fifty years of unjust government will not be wiped away by a few tentative and marginal efforts at greater participation for the minority. It is too late for that. Concessions which might have helped twenty or ten, or even five years ago, are only drops of water sprinkled into a furnace now. On the side of the minority there has got to be acceptance of the fact that any effort to try to force changes in the basic constitutional position of Northern Ireland in the present situation can only increase the likelihood of conflict and decrease the possibilities of achieving social and political equality

In the present situation there is not the slightest possibility of gaining the consent of a majority in Northern Ireland for fundamental constitutional change. Therefore, such change could only be brought about by coercion of that majority. That could not be done without extreme violence.

Only when a normal, just, democratic society, based on full equality for all citizens has been established in Northern Ireland will it be possible to think in terms of seeking consent for constitutional change.

The promoting of agreement, and the avoidance of a bloody intercommunal struggle in Northern Ireland, rest jointly with the British and Irish Governments. It would be well for the British Government to recognise this clearly. The Irish Government has it within its power to prevent any solution which it does not accept, or which the minority in Northern Ireland does not accept. No constitutional position in Northern Ireland can be made viable without the consent of the Irish Government. If any lingering illusions still remain with the British Government that it can solve the Northern Ireland problem on its own by the use of its army for pacification, or by any other military or political means, then it had better drop those illusions quickly. The fact that we are where we are after fifty years is the most conclusive proof there could be that this problem cannot be solved by the British Government alone.

The final shape of a settlement of the Northern Ireland problem must involve a continuing joint guarantee by the Irish and British Governments of equality of rights and full social justice for every citizen in Northern Ireland. It must involve a joint responsibility by the two Governments to create and maintain a new constitutional position acceptable to a majority in Northern Ireland and a majority in the Republic. If that responsibility were unambiguously assumed by both Governments jointly, and if at the same time there were a clear and total commitment against extremists on both sides, then we would be faced at least in the right direction for finding a solution, even if the process of evolving one was still a long painful and frustrating one.

Nationalism and European Unity[1]

Michael Sweetman

The result of the referendum on the Common Market in May will have a profound effect on the prospects for future Irish unity. The implications of the vote for this issue are not always fully understood in Ireland. This is a field where emotion too often substitutes for logical thought.

One harsh fact not often faced is that even if, by some miracle, agreement could be reached today on an all-Ireland state, there would be some tough economic problems to surmount. The Westminster Treasury guarantees Northern farmers higher incomes than their Southern brethren enjoy. All Northern citizens enjoy a much higher standard of social service—again subsidised from Westminster. If these standards were to be provided for North and South by an All-Ireland Government, it would mean an enormous increase in taxation—at least an extra £200 million or more than one third of the present total national budget. There are (or at least were until recently) many Catholics in Northern Ireland who would have been reluctant to accept national unity at a cost of substantially lower living standards.

The prospect of EEC membership radically alters this. EEC membership would, over the years 1973–1978, automatically eliminate any difference in income between Northern and Southern farmers. During this period, incomes of Southern farmers would rise steeply, while at the same time the subsidies (now amounting to about 6 per cent of the total national budget) paid to them by the Dublin Government would no longer be needed and would be available for improving social services. This should go a long way towards progressively eliminating present economic disparities between North and South. This process would be further helped by the complete elimination of customs barriers on both sides, harmonisation of tax systems and

1 *The Tablet* March 1972

ultimately of tax rates, and increasing use of European Community resources to aid development of the less developed areas both North and South of the border. Some of the country's most serious develop- ment problems are in border areas and exist to some extent because of the frontier which artificially divides natural economic regions—the North-West is an outstanding example, with Donegal cut off from its natural centre Derry. A development plan for the North-West would have to include areas both sides of the border.

There are, then, very solid economic reasons why EEC member- ship will help ease divisions within the country. Some political effects, while being less tangible, will be equally important. Many of the is- sues with which we will be concerned in Brussels will be of equal concern to Northern Ireland. One can think of issues—agriculture, for example, or regional development—where the United Kingdom government, being concerned with a much wider area than Northern Ireland, may not always fully reflect in its policy the special interests of Northern Ireland. In that situation, Northern interests will find increasingly that, because their needs coincide with those of the rest of Ireland, the Irish Government representatives will be their most effective spokesmen. This emergence of mutual interest in the Euro- pean arena must promote a greater awareness of what the country as a whole has in common, and somewhat less emphasis on traditional divisions which will seem less and less relevant. The sense of com- mon Irishness is always enhanced when Irishmen, however diverse their backgrounds, find themselves together in the presence of other nationalities.

This line of argument is, of course, rejected by the more extreme kind of nationalist. First of all, it savours too much of acceptance of the existing border. These groups think in terms of a revolution which will sweep away the division at one stroke, rather than a peaceful evo- lution over a long period. But, of course, this kind of daydreaming about an instantaneous solution has never in the past produced any practical progress towards healing the real divisions of which the bor- der is only a symptom—in fact, as most people recognise, violence has merely deepened these divisions.

Most reasonable people recognise that the only meaningful or ac- ceptable kind of Irish unity would be one based on a genuine rec- onciliation between the Protestants of the North and the Catholic community, North and South. Despite its lofty protestations and progressive sounding policies, this view is not in fact accepted by so-called 'republicanism'. This 'republicanism' is really a kind of aggressive nationalism which by its actions, as opposed to its words, consistently shows that it does not recognise as valid any cultural norms or traditions except its own. Its attitude to the North-East has consistently been 'you have no right to be different. If you insist on being different then we, acting on behalf of our concept of the Irish nation (essentially Gaelic and Catholic) have the right to kill you, drive you out or condemn you to second-class citizenship'. If this seems harsh, we should remember that, at least since 1937, the South has lived under laws and a constitution which reflect this mentality—whether in the attempts to impose the Gaelic language and culture on everybody, or the primacy given to Catholic attitudes and teaching.

The ideal of European unity is an effort to break away from the various nationalisms which have done such incalculable harm to the peoples of Europe over the past century. Nationalism, when it bursts through as a desire to kill and destroy others (as it has done in Ireland no less than in every other part of Western Europe), is a vicious thing. Fifty million dead in Europe this century are mute witnesses to that. Too often we have confused patriotism, a legitimate love of one's homeland, with nationalism, which so often shows as a hatred of others. It is my belief that in learning to live and work constructively with the other peoples of Europe, we in Ireland will learn to live in peace with each other.

Speech to the New York
Athletic Club[1]

Michael Sweetman

Ladies and Gentlemen, I want to tell you first how much I appreciate your invitation to me to come here this evening and tell you something of recent developments in Ireland.

I must admit that I feel a certain diffidence in talking to Americans about Ireland in terms of development or progress. I have the feeling that many of you like to think of Ireland as a kind of crazy legendary fairyland, uncomplicated by the complexities of life in the age of the internal combustion engine and the atom. I hate to spoil your fantasy. You think of Ireland perhaps as a place which it is fun to dream about and romance about, but not really a place where modern man could seriously think of living. I met someone here recently whose mother had left Ireland as a girl of about twelve and was just back in the United States from a visit to her homeland fifty years later. Apparently what impressed her more than anything else on getting off the plane was the fact that there were motor cars in Ireland. She had apparently expected to see everybody going about in the donkey carts and side cars which she remembered from the turn of the century.

This admittedly is an extreme example, but it does illustrate very well what has been described by someone as the 'green curtain' which veils modern Ireland from the age of our American cousins. The 'green curtain', as you will have noticed in the past few weeks, is heavily hung with clay pipes, green hats, plastic shillelaghs made in Japan and other paraphernalia connected with St Patrick's Day revelry. You will hardly believe me when I say that, although I have lived all my life in Ireland, I never saw a shillelagh until I came to North America some five years ago, while the only clay pipes I ever saw were those sold to children for blowing bubbles and even those, I suppose, have been replaced by

1 Sunday 17 March 1963

bubblegum, in which incidentally we do a thriving export trade.

What the Irish ask, more than anything else, of Americans today is to be taken seriously. While the Irishman has a justifiable reputation for his wit and humour, he gets a little tired at times at being taken for a clown and this aversion to being thought of as a clown is not just the result of vanity. It is of very practical importance to him. My function in this country, for instance, is to promote the sale of Irish products in America. You will easily understand that my efforts and the efforts of our exporters when we try to interest Americans in our fabrics, our fashions, our foods and our drinks, are not helped by the belief of many Americans that Ireland is a primitive country and could not possible produce anything which a modern man or woman would want to wear or use. Even our whiskey enjoys a quite unjustifiable reputation for excess alcoholic strength and coarseness whereas, of course, as its devotees know, it has a rather lower proof strength than many American whiskies.

The mention of whiskey reminds of the story of the three whiskey salesmen who met in a bar at lunch one day. One of them sold bourbon, the other Scotch, the third Irish. The bourbon salesman made a point of ordering bourbon while the scotch salesman made a point of ordering scotch, but when they asked the Irish salesman what he would have, he said it made no difference to him—he'd have either bourbon or Scotch—anything, so long as it wasn't Irish.

'Well, you're a fine salesman,' the others taunted him, 'you won't even drink your own product yourself.'

'Well, the way it is you see,' the Irish salesman explained, 'I don't like to go in after lunch to see a customer with a smell of whiskey on my breath.'

In any case, I am happy to say that, despite the 'green curtain', sales of our products in the United States have more than quadrupled over the last five years. I won't burden you with the details but will just mention that these exports including such a wide variety of things as beef, footwear, whiskey, fabric, fancy foods and women's fashions, are now featured in many of the best stores in America.

I have spoken of the 'green curtain' and what we in Ireland sometimes think of as the rather unfortunate illusions which Americans have about Ireland. I should perhaps try and give you some idea of what Ireland today is really like.

Ireland seems to me today to be an ideal blend of the simple, more leisurely, past with the comforts and convenience of the 20th century. What makes life in, say, Dublin essentially different from life in New York, is, I think, its simplicity. A man living in Dublin has all the comforts and conveniences of a modern city but without the complexities and proverbial high pressure of an enormous urban area like New York. It will, I think, illustrate what I mean when I say that you can drive in well under half an hour of leisurely driving from the centre of Dublin into the depths of the country to a good fishing river, perhaps, where there is nobody else in sight—or to one of the many superb golf courses which are all around the outskirts of the city. There are no such things as traffic jams on Irish roads, although we have nothing comparable to your great thruways and turnpikes. Driving there is a quiet, leisurely operation with plenty of time to enjoy the scenery around you. Scenery which, by the way, changes at every twist and turn of the road. To go out fishing or hunting, for example, you don't have to make an expedition of it. If the humour takes you some afternoon, you simply throw your rod or gun into the back of the car and you are there in a matter of minutes ready for action; and despite the fact that Ireland is such a small country you will likely have the place to yourself.

They tell a story about a visitor from New York who went to Ireland for some salmon fishing. This visitor wasn't much good at fishing but succeeding in catching one salmon—and even that was practically tied on to the end of the line for him by the boatman, but the visitor blamed his failure on the teeming loch rather than on himself.

'Hell,' he complained to the boatman, 'this beauty has cost me more than $500.'

'Well, if it cost you that much,' answered the boatman innocently, 'aren't you the lucky one that you didn't catch more of them.'

In recent years, of course, the Irish Government has been making a tremendous effort to develop industry in Ireland in order to provide work for those who, in keeping with the worldwide trend, are abandoning farming in favour of industrial work. To attract outside capitalists, the Irish Government has been offering very generous grants towards the costs of establishing new industries as well as special tax privileges, which in many cases, amount to complete tax exemption on profits for many years. There are no restrictions on the withdrawal of these profits from Ireland, although we naturally like to see them reinvested in the country. This policy has been very successful and as a result of the establishment of hundreds of new industries over the last few years, gives valuable employment to thousands of people who would otherwise have had to emigrate. So successful has their policy been, in fact, that the numbers of people emigrating from Ireland have fallen dramatically in recent years and it is even expected that over the next decade Ireland will show a net increase in population, thus reversing a long established trend. We would incidentally very much like to see more American capitalists investing in Ireland, which, apart from the grants and tax privileges already mentioned, offers them political stability and a tremendous fund of goodwill which is hard to find in other parts of the world today.

There are those who fear that the industrialisation of Ireland would spoil the unique character of the country and its people. This fear, I am glad to say, has turned out to be quite unfounded. The new industries are well spread through the country and discreetly located so as not to detract from the famous scenery. There is even a crane factory in Killarney, but unless you went to look for it you would not know it was there. This policy of bringing factories to the people, rather than the people to the factories, leaves the traditional pattern of Irish country life relatively undisturbed and those who once would have had to leave their homes to go and work in the industrial cities of England, or indeed of the United States, can now make a good living in their own town or village.

Ireland is, today, as a result of all this, more prosperous than she's ever been before. It is worth mentioning in this connection that Ireland does not seek one penny of foreign aid from the United States or any other country and does not intend to do so in the future. We feel that the enthusiasm and resourcefulness of our own people, allied with private investors from overseas can achieve the development which we want for our country.

Among other things, I have heard it said that you can sleep better in Ireland than anywhere else in the world—an important point for those returning from a hectic tour of Europe. And so between American businessmen investing there, American tourists visiting us and our own efforts to spread the good word of the United States we hope that the 'green curtain' with its clowning leprechauns and shillelagh swinging boyos will finally be thrown where it belongs, on the rubbish heap.

Ireland and the Common Market[1]

Michael Sweetman

T he motives of Britain and Ireland in joining the EEC are very different, indeed in some respects opposite. For example, economically the biggest attraction for Ireland is participation in the EEC agricultural policy. This will mean a near doubling of income for many farmers producing beef, lamb and milk, while simultaneously relieving the Irish Government of a large part of the almost £100m or about 20 per cent of the total national budget which it now pays in subsidies and other aids to farmers. These subsidies have been necessary because Britain, pursuing her cheap food policy, has consistently forced Ireland to accept uneconomically low prices for agricultural produce. This neo-colonialist relationship will be eliminated by EEC membership. The effect on the Irish economy is expected by supporters of membership to be dramatic—at least 20,000 new jobs as a result of expansion of the agriculture-based industries and the higher purchasing power of farmers. About 28 per cent of Ireland's workforce is still in agriculture, compared with 2 per cent in Britain.

No such dramatic gains are expected by industry, although on balance most of Irish industry favours EEC membership if only because if Britain joined and Ireland stayed out, this would cause even more severe disruption than anything threatened by membership. In any case, the main free trade threat to Irish industry comes from the Anglo-Irish Free Trade Area Agreement under which all tariffs between Britain and Ireland will be removed by mid-1975, while under the proposed transition period to EEC membership high tariffs will still remain against EEC countries for a year or two after this. Early in the 1960s detailed studies by Government and industry estimated that up to 10,000 out of the total of about 200,000 jobs in Irish industry

[1] Commissioned by *The Times* in July 1971 for a Special Report on the Republic of Ireland

might be lost as a result of removing protection. Since then there has been a good deal of preparation by industry (although the effectiveness of some of it is disputed) and this employment loss should be somewhat reduced. Increased investment in new industrial development, as well as the new job opportunities already mentioned, should more than compensate for these losses.

The economic case for Irish membership, therefore, seems pretty clear cut, particularly with Britain joining. Those in Ireland who oppose membership have suggested some form of trade agreement as an alternative and point to the efforts of countries like Sweden, Switzerland, Austria and Finland to get the benefits without assuming the obligations of membership. The difficulty about a trade agreement from the Irish point of view is that it must inevitably apply mainly to industrial goods—the aspect of EEC membership where we have least to gain. Not even the most optimistic advocates of this alternative claim that the Community would give us significant access to Community markets at Community prices for our main agricultural products, particularly milk. A trade agreement would, therefore, give us the same unfavourable economic relationship with the EEC which we now have with Britain. We would, in effect, have to take all the disadvantages of free competition in industrial goods, while gaining none of the advantages of high prices and guaranteed markets for agriculture. We would also miss out on help with development under EEC regional policy.

Opponents of EEC membership have tried, not I think very successfully, to discount the obvious attractions of membership to the farming community by claiming that the favourable conditions for agriculture will not last and that the effect of EEC agricultural policy if applied to Ireland would be to drastically reduce the numbers of people on the land. This argument is weak in that it is not easy to see how greatly increased incomes for most farmers can result in their leaving the land faster than they are now doing—the opposite should be the logical effect. Furthermore, all the evidence is that farmers within the Community already have enough political power to maintain their incomes at least at present levels for the foreseeable future. Because Irish climatic and soil conditions make grassland farming much more economic here than in most parts of Europe, Irish farmers are confident that any price level which will keep Continental farmers alive will give them a very comfortable living.

In reality, most of the argument against EEC membership is basically political rather than economic—the implication is that the political reasons for remaining out are so pressing that some economic sacrifice is justified in order to do so. This political opposition has several sources. Firstly, the widespread unpopularity of the present Government, and doubts as to its competence leave many people uneasy about whether it really knows what it is doing. This uneasiness is not helped by the fact that the decision to apply for full membership was taken as far back as 1961 without any real public debate. In fact, popular debate only really got started in the last two years and the Government, by coming into this discussion with its mind already made up for many years, has given the impression of not being prepared to examine alternatives in a reasonably objective way. Membership has become an article of establishment orthodoxy, with all the provocation to radically-minded people which that involves.

More explicit opposition to membership comes essentially from right-wing nationalist groups, such as the two factions of Sinn Féin and from the extreme Left—the latter being influenced by the line taken for many years by Moscow and some of the West-European communist parties. The small Irish Labour Party (16 out of 144 seats in the Dáil) also officially opposes membership although a number of its leading personalities are known to favour membership and to be unhappy with this stand.

The extreme nationalist groups (which have had very little electoral support in recent years) are concerned that national independence may be compromised. The extreme Left are worried that participation in what they feel is an essentially capitalist-dominated group will delay the Revolution. The Labour Party's position is largely based on expediency. With the main Opposition Party supporting membership it seemed attractive to take the lead in opposing the Referendum on membership which the Irish constitution makes necessary. The latest opinion polls suggest a 2 to 1 vote in this referendum in favour of membership but the Labour Party presumably hopes to retain the subsequent political allegiance of at least some of those who vote No.

One widely shared concern about membership is that it will involve entanglement in the military policies of the major European powers. Most people in Ireland, including the vast majority of 'Europeans' will strongly oppose any such involvement.

A country which has enjoyed independence for such a short time and after such a bitter struggle, is naturally sensitive to any loss of sovereignty. However, those in favour of EEC membership argue that, while enjoying nominal independence, Ireland at present has very little real power to use it. Whether in political or economic affairs the decisions of the larger countries, and in our case most obviously Britain, vitally affect our interests and as things now stand we have neither right nor power to participate in or influence those decisions.

Membership of the Community, by contrast, has special attractions for the small country which sees the power of its big neighbours brought under Community control and its own rights defined and protected by agreed institutions. The right to be heard and to have one's interests taken into account when decisions are being taken is of inestimable value to the small country. The importance which Luxembourg has acquired since becoming a member of the EEC has not gone unnoticed here, nor has the fact that it is the smaller EEC members who consistently show most enthusiasm for maintaining and indeed extending it.

In summary, there are compelling economic reasons for Ireland to seek full membership of the Community, particularly if Britain joins. On the other hand, there is general concern about loss of sovereignty and the danger of being pushed about by bureaucrats from Brussels. As against this, the EEC concept seems to offer a small country like Ireland new opportunities for political initiative and participation in decision-taking at European level.

A 'European' foreign policy[1]

Michael Sweetman

Practically all discussion about the EEC in this country has so far centred around the economic implications of membership for industry and agriculture. This is unfortunate, because the political implications of membership are just as important, and in fact it is likely to be our political attitude rather than our economic problems which will determine the success or failure of our application for membership, or at least the extent to which we can secure satisfactory solutions to our economic problems.

We think and talk so much about our own economic affairs that it is easy to forget how insignificant in scale these are when set against the scale of the EEC—a community with a total population well over 200 million (including Britain) against our mere two and three quarter million. Economically, then, Irish membership would have virtually no significance for the EEC and the Community would have no serious difficulty in making whatever economic arrangements were necessary to satisfy our reasonable requirements—if it wanted to.

This is where our political attitudes are of vital importance. We have nothing to offer the Community economically, but we have politically something of potential value to offer. We are the only Western European country with[out] a colonial past. We pioneered the world movement against colonialism, and this gives us a certain position with the newly independent countries of Africa and Asia which is not shared by any other European power. If we show a willingness to place our special relationship to the so-called 'Third World' at the service of a European foreign policy we will be offering the community something which it would regard as cheap at the price of whatever economic arrangements were necessary to ensure our continued and growing material prosperity within the Community.

What is implied in the term 'European foreign policy'? In very broad terms the Community is moving towards a policy of much greater independence of American policies and attitudes than has

[1] *The Citizen* 13 November 1971

been possible since the last war. For example, the United States is both a Pacific and an Atlantic power and in its current scale of priorities the tendency is for its Pacific interests to take precedence over those of Europe. Europe, on the other hand, has since the war disentangled itself completely from political responsibility and interests in Asia. Britain, which still has pretensions to a role East of Suez, is likely to have to abandon this as part of any deal for membership of the EEC because the Continental European countries, having disentangled themselves from what they claim to regard as unprofitable interests in Asia, have no intention of becoming involved again in political and military responsibilities which do not appear to serve any European interest. As Germany has proved since the war, trade no longer has to have a flag to follow and in the post-colonial era influence and good-will are more effectively promoted by keeping out of other people's affairs rather than meddling in them, however high-minded the mo-tives for interference may be.

The EEC countries are concentrating their attention on the prob-lems of Europe. This means increasing concern with seeking a long-term accommodation with Russia. Russia and the other countries of Eastern Europe have for centuries been part of the European family of nations. There is a growing desire within the EEC for the breaking down of the Iron Curtain, not just to re-unite Germany but to restore the historic unity of Europe from the Atlantic to the Urals.

In the eyes of many Europeans this goal is at present being imped-ed by American activities in Asia. In particular, most Europeans do not share America's obsession with fighting Communism and, in the light of liberalising trends in Eastern Europe and devolving attitudes within the EEC, see the ideological division of Europe into Commu-nist and non-Communist parts as increasingly irrelevant. It is widely believed that only a Europe which is completely free of commitment to American policies of the kind which have led to the present appall-ing situation in Vietnam (widely disapproved of in Europe) can reach a real understanding with the Soviet bloc.

So far the Irish Government has shown little understanding of this. Our Minister for External Affairs spends most of his time in New York promoting policies which not only have little relevance to European interests but are, on occasion, contrary to the policy of the most powerful member of the EEC. Our present activities in the field of foreign affairs are relevant only within the framework of American concepts and aspirations.

By following them we run the very serious risk of being lumped together in the European mind with those very policies and attitudes of the British which earned them the accusation of not being 'European' enough for membership of the EEC. Nothing could be more disastrous for our prospects of successful negotiations for membership of the Community.

In shaping our foreign policy and, in particular, in using the 'considerable political influence' which we have in the world, and which is out of all proportion to our size or economic importance, we must, very consciously and deliberately, align ourselves with European thought and attitudes rather than with the 'Anglo-Saxons'. If we seriously want to join the EEC we must become 'European' in the only field in which we have anything to contribute to the Community in exchange for the economic benefits we are going to seek from it. We are unlikely to be accepted as a good European until our Minister for External Affairs is seen to be spending far more time in the capitals of Europe than in New York, or anywhere else that his ambitious, well-meaning but, in our present situation, dangerously irrelevant policies may lead him.

Index